Hebrew:
BEGINNING YOUR JOURNEY

MARY A. MERRITT

DR. D. MICHAEL MICHAEL, EDITOR

Olive Press Messianic and Christian Publisher

The main Hebrew font in this book is BWHEBB, Postscript®
TrueTypeT font Copyright © 1994-2011 BibleWorks, LLC.
All rights reserved. This Biblical Hebrew font is used with
permission and is from BibleWorks (www.bibleworks.com).
This copyright notice must be displayed when using this font.

Unlabeled Scripture quotations are from The Interlinear
Hebrew-Greek-English Bible, Vol. I, 1980, by Jay P. Green, Sr.,
and are used with the permission of Jay Green, Jr.

Scripture quotations marked "NKJV™" are taken from the New
King James Version®. Copyright © 1982 by Thomas Nelson, Inc.
Used by permission. All rights reserved.

Scriptures marked "KJV" are taken from the King James Version.
Psalms 34, 111, and 145 are based on the KJV. The word order has been changed in some cases.
The Hebrew portion of these Psalms is used with permission, from Biblia Hebraica Stuttgartensia,
edited by Karl Elliger and Wilhelm Rudolph, Fifth Revised Edition, edited by Adrian Schenker,
© 1977 and 1997 Deutsche Bibelgesellschaft, Stuttgart.

Watercolor illustrations by Melissa Merritt

Cover design by Ann Merritt

Inside design by Ann and Mary Merritt

ISBN 978-0-9855241-9-7

In Memory of

my beloved husband,

Keith Irvin Merritt,

who entered into the presence of the Lord

on Seventh Day, September 9, 2006.

This book is humbly dedicated to

the Lord Jesus, the Messiah

and Savior of all who believe in Him

for the forgiveness of their sins. He is the

"Alpha and Omega," or the "Alef and the Tahv,"

if you will, the "Beginning and the End."

"Not unto us, O LORD, not unto us,

but unto Thy name give glory,

for Thy mercy, and for Thy truth's sake."

Psalm 115:1 KJV

TABLE OF CONTENTS

FOREWORD

God is truly a God of miracles. He has kept the Jewish people alive without a homeland for 2000 years, while many people groups wanted to exterminate them. He gave Israel back to the Jewish people in 1948. He allowed Israel to be victorious in war with their neighbors who surrounded them, though the Jewish people sought to live in peace. He allowed Jerusalem to be restored to Jewish hands. Recently, God has brought many Jewish people to receive Yeshua (Jesus) as their Messiah, and He has brought many Christians to once again search for their foundational understanding of Scripture – through Jewish eyes as they realize that Jesus and His disciples were Jewish.

One of the miracles that God performed in the late 19th century was the revival of the Hebrew language. This revival has generated a new and great interest in learning Hebrew. Hebrew is not just for Israelis, nor is it only for Bar & Bat Mitzvah students. Hebrew is for all of us who want to know better how to "handle accurately the Word of Truth."

Hebrew: Beginning Your Journey, by Mary A. Merritt, is a great way for young and old to start the journey of learning Hebrew. It makes great sense. The pictures are informative and visually inspiring. Tying the Hebrew to the Scriptures is motivating and extremely helpful in "hiding the Word in our hearts."

The logical progression in this book makes the learning of Hebrew attainable.

You have what you need to step-by-step get to the next level: lesson plans, assignments, quizzes, writing practice – the list goes on and on.

This is a journey worth taking. May God bless you and your family as you experience the joys of learning Hebrew.

Rabbi Steven J. Weiler
Tampa, FL

LESSON PLANS FOR THE YEAR: HOW TO USE THIS BOOK

These lesson plans will be a necessary guide to your study. They are laid out with forty weeks of the year in mind. Be sure to follow the instructions *carefully* for each week! Color in the stars below when you complete each of the directions. *A slow, steady, and consistent study will be most productive and well worth the more thorough effort! The emphasis should be upon careful mastery of all the information contained in each week's lesson.* Do not move ahead unless you know the lesson well. Do not worry about how long it takes you!

WEEK 1 (When each direction below is completed, *check off by shading in the Star of David.* ✡)

✡ **Practice writing** only the letters *alef, bet, gimel,* and *dalet* on the "Practice Pages For the Hebrew Alef-Bet," pp. 67-70, but complete only the top section! (You will come back to the bottom half in later weeks.)

✡ **Practice (on your own paper)**, these letters again, always reciting the names and sounds of the letters as you write.

✡ **Create flash cards** for these first four letters. **Save these cards** from week to week until you have all 22 letters of the alef-bet. It will be helpful to have notebook with "pockets" to store these.

✡ **Memorize** the first four letters, i.e., to say in order, to read and write them, to know their sounds.

✡ **Recite** the first four letters to other family members.

✡ **Learn to say** the greeting for "Good morning!" in Hebrew. Say "Bo-kehr tohv!" בֹּקֶר טוֹב ⇐ We start reading from right to left!

WEEKS 2-3

✡ **Read and Study** the information in the "Notes on the Hebrew Alef-Bet," p. 55, for *alef, bet, gimel,* and *dalet*, the first four letters of the alef-bet.

✡ **Recite** the first four letters. Make this a daily practice! Be able to not only recite them, but READ them and know their sounds!

✡ **Study** all the word pictures on the Alef Picture Page, p. 3. Sound out the words, using the pronunciation helps in parentheses. The word for "father" is "ah-bah." אָ (ah), + בָ (bah) + א (silent, no vowel)= אַבָּא (ah-bah), reading from right to left and top to bottom.

✡ **Create** your own pictures for at least two of the words on the Alef Picture Page, p. 3. These are to go into your own "abecedary" (book of ABCs). We suggest that you cut a standard 8x11 sheet of paper in half for your two pictures (but it is up to you to decide how large you want to make your book.) Be creative! You may want to use photographs, picture cutouts to paste on the page, or your own sketches or paintings. Feel free to include a photograph of your own father and mother for "abba" and "eemah." **Label** the Hebrew word next to your picture. **Save** pictures in a folder from week to week and when completed (at the end of the year), staple or tie your book together and make a cover.

LESSON PLANS—WEEKS 4-5 (Shade in the Star of David when you finish each assignment.)

✡ **Read and study** the "Notes," p. 56, for *hay, vahv,* and *zayin.*

✡ **Practice writing** *hay, vahv,* and *zayin* on the Practice Pages, pp. 71-73, **only the top of the page.**

✡ **Practice writing these letters again** on your own paper, notating or reciting the names and sounds associated with them.

✡ **Create flash cards** for *hay, vahv,* and *zayin.* Put all cards together from *alef - zayin* and scramble them up and put them in order again. Make a game of this!

✡ **Memorize** these three new letters.

✡ **Recite** the first seven letters of the Hebrew alef-bet, over and over!

✡ **Study** all the word pictures for the letter *bet,* p. 5, reading with pronunciation guides until you understand.

✡ **Create** at least two pictures from the picture page for *bet.* **Label** and **add** to your file for your own "abecedary" book.

✡ **Learn to say** the Bible verse, Genesis 1:1 in Hebrew. It is found on p. 103.

WEEKS 6-7

✡ **Study** the "Notes" for *khet, tet, yud* and *kaf,* p. 57.

✡ **Practice writing** *khet, tet, yud, kaf/khaf* on Practice Pages, pp. 74-77 (single letters at the top). The remaining part will be done in a later week.

✡ **Practice writing these letters again** on your own paper, reciting their names and sounds.

✡ **Create flash cards** for these letters. Add with the first letters, scramble, and put in order again.

✡ **Memorize** these four new letters.

✡ **Recite** all the letters from *alef to kaf.*

✡ **Study the pictures** on the *gimel* page, p. 7, always sounding out the Hebrew words, with helps from Nikood Sound System, p. 49.

✡ **Create two pictures** for *gimel* words of your choice, **label** with Hebrew words, and **add** to your file for your abecedary.

✡ **Review** and recite Genesis 1:1 in Hebrew.

✡ **Learn** the greeting for "Good day!" in Hebrew. Say "Yohm tohv!" יוֹם טוֹב and practice it on your family.

WEEKS 8-9

✡ **Study** the "Notes" for *lamed, mem, nun,* and *samek,* pp. 58-59.

✡ **Practice writing** the single letters for *lamed, mem, nun,* and *samek* on Practice Pages, pp. 78-81.

✡ **Practice writing these letters again** on your own paper, reciting names and sounds.

✡ **Create flash cards.** Play the scramble game with these four letters, and then with all letters from *alef* through *samek.*

✡ **Memorize** these letters in order.

✡ **Recite** all letters learned so far. You are over half way there!

✡ **Study pictures** for the *dalet* picture page, p. 9, sounding out Hebrew words.

✡ **Create** your own version of pictures that begin with *dalet,* as on p. 9. **Label** and **add** to your file.

✡ **Reading Practice,** p. 89. Write the sounds (pronunciations) for each letter on the blank lines.

✡ **Learn to say** the phrase for "Good night!" Say "LIE-lah tohv!" לַיְלָה טוֹב Write it on paper.

✡ **Practice** saying the Hebrew for "Good night!" to your friends.

✡ **Read and Study** the pages for *ayin, pay/fay* and *tsadee* on the "Notes," page 59.

✡ **Practice writing** *ayin, pay/fay,* and *tsadee* on the Practice Pages, pp. 82-84, but only the single letters at the top of the page.

✡ **Practice writing on your own paper** again, reciting the names and sounds they make.

✡ **Create flash cards** for *ayin, pay/fay* and *tsadee*. Play Scramble game with flash cards.

✡ **Memorize** these letters in order.

✡ **Recite** all letters in order learned so far.

✡ **Study the pictures** and words for *hay*, p. 11, sounding out the Hebrew words.

✡ **Create pictures** of your own for two or more of the words on the *hay* picture page, p. 11. **Label** and **add** to your abecedary file.

✡ **Copy Quiz 1** from p. 98. Using the copy, **take the quiz.** (You will take this quiz again later, in the book.) You may look for the answers from the Picture Pages in the front of this book. Use the answer key, p. 113, as a last resort only, after you have searched the picture pages!

✡ **Sound out** the **Reading Practice** exercises on p. 90, and fill in the blank lines.

WEEKS 11-12

✡ **Read and Study** the "Notes," p. 60, for *kuf, reysh, seen/sheen* and *tahv.*

✡ **Practice writing** *kuf, reysh, seen/sheen* and *tahv* on Writing Practice Pages, pp. 85-88.

✡ **Practice on your own paper** these letters again, reciting names and sounds.

✡ **Create flash cards** for these letters. Scramble and put in order. Play Scramble game with all 22 letters of the alef-bet.

✡ **Memorize** these new letters.

✡ **Recite** *alef* through *tahv* to family members.

✡ **Turn to page 71,** "Practice Page for Hay." In the middle of the page, write the word for "mountain."

✡ **Study** the words on Picture Page for the letter *vahv*, p. 13.

✡ **Create** your own pictures for *vahv*. **Label** them and **add** to the abecedary file.

✡ **Go to the Practice Page** for *alef*, p. 67. **Fill in** the *bottom* of the page, doing neat, accurate work.

✡ Learn these words. You can make pictures of these words and add to your abecedary also.

✡ Can you still say Genesis 1:1? **Review** your verse every day!

✡ **Learn Bible Memory Verse** - Deuteronomy 6:4. It is on p. 103.

✡ **Turn to "Can You Find the ABCs?"** on p. 50. This is the first of the alphabetical Psalms. **Read the instructions** and then do the exercise.

WEEKS 13-14

✡ **Writing Practice Pages** for *bet* and *gimel* pp. 68, 69. Finish the *bottom* half of these pages.

✡ **Recite** the whole alef-bet every day! Can you say it all within 45 seconds? Time yourself.

✡ **Play** the Scramble game with all 22 flash card letters.

✡ **Study** the pictures on the *zayin* page, p. 15, always sounding out the Hebrew words.

✡ **Create** your own pictures for the *zayin* words. **Label** with Hebrew words, and **add** to your file.

✡ **Review and recite** Deuteronomy 6:4 in Hebrew. Also review Genesis 1:1.

✡ **Take Quiz 1** (p. 98) again in pencil, this time in the book, **without** looking up the answers.

✡ **Read and follow the directions** for Psalm 111, "Can You Find the ABCs? No. 2," p. 52.

✡ **Do the exercises** for **Reading Practice**, p. 91.

LESSON PLANS—WEEKS 15-16 (Shade in the Star of David when you finish each assignment.)

✡ **Practice writing** the words at the bottom of the Practice Pages for *dalet* and *hay*, pp. 70, 71.

✡ **Recite** the whole alef-bet. Write it in order on your own paper.

✡ **Play** the Scramble game with flash cards.

✡ **Study pictures** for the *khet* page, p. 17.

✡ **Create pictures** for *khet*. **Label** and **add** to your abecedary file.

✡ **Read** and follow directions for "Can You Find the ABCs? No. 3," pp. 53, 54

✡ **Take Matching Quiz 1**, p. 92. Be sure to sound out/read the Hebrew words as you go along.

✡ **Learn** to say and read the question, "How are you?" (To a male: Ma shlom-KHAH?) ? מַה שְׁלוֹמְךָ
and, "How are you?" (To a female: Ma shlo-MECH?) ? מַה שְׁלוֹמֵךְ
(This literally means "How is your peace?" See p. 105 of Common Expressions.)

WEEKS 17-18

✡ **Practice writing** *vahv* and *zayin* on the Practice Pages, pp. 72, 73. Complete the pages.

✡ **Play** Scramble game with your flash cards.

✡ **Recite** all letters in order. Are you getting faster at recitation, and still having accuracy?

✡ **Study** the pictures and words for *tet*, p. 19.

✡ **Create pictures** for two or more of the words on the *tet* page, p. 19. **Label** and add to your abecedary.

✡ **Copy Quiz 2** (fill in the blanks quiz) on p. 99. After you make a copy, **take the quiz** the first time.
Do not write answers in the book until you take the test again in Week 21. You may look up the answers
from the Picture Pages in the front of this book. Use the answer key, p. 113, as a last resort only.

✡ **Review** Bible verses Genesis 1:1 and Deuteronomy 6:4, p. 103.

✡ **Learn** the most common answer to "How are you?," which is, "Everything is just fine." (Literally,
"Blessed is the Lord.") (Bah-ruch Ha-shem.) בָּרוּךְ הַשֵׁם
Other answers you might use are: "Fine."(b'-SAY-dehr); בְּסֵדֶר
and, "Very well, thank you!" (tohv m'-OHD, toh-DAH rah-BAH!) טוֹב מְאֹד תּוֹדָה רַבָּה

WEEKS 19-20

✡ **Practice writing** *khet* and *tet* on the Practice Pages, pp. 74, 75. Fill in the **bottom** of the pages.

✡ **Play** Scramble game with all 22 letters of the alef-bet.

✡ **Study** the words on Picture Page for *yud*, p. 21.

✡ **Create** your own pictures for *yud*. **Label** them and add to the abecedary.

✡ **Take Matching Quiz 2**, p. 93. Sound out the words carefully.

✡ **Read** page 107, **the VERB "TO BE."** Follow directions, fill in blanks.

✡ **Read/study** "Alef-bet of Verbs," p. 61. Follow the directions for the *alef* and *bet* verbs .

✡ Try to memorize one verb a week. Also make a flash card for each verb.

✡ **Begin making a new List of Vocabulary Words**, including these verbs. Keep reviewing and testing
yourself on them. I strongly suggest that you make both a list of desired vocabulary words
(as you come across them,) as well as an alphabetized (dictionary-form) list of Hebrew words.

✡ **Then make flash cards** for each word you add. (The more times you write the Hebrew words,
the longer you will remember them!)

✡ **Have a family member test you** with the word flash cards.

✡ **Learn** some more "Common Expressions," p. 105.

✡ **Recite** the alef-bet. Can you say it within 30 seconds?

✡ **Fill in** the bottom of the Practice Pages for *yud* and *kaf*, pp. 76, 77.

✡ **Study** the pictures for the *kaf* page, p. 23.

✡ **Draw** your own pictures, **label** and **add** to your file for your own abecedary.

✡ **Take Quiz 2** (fill in the blank), p. 99, this time in the book, trying NOT to look up answers.

✡ **Learn new verse** from the Tanach, Isaiah 6:3. See Bible Memory Verses, p. 103, WEEK 21, for the spelling and pronunciation.

✡ **See "Alef-bet of Verbs,"** p. 62. Learn verb roots for *gimel* and *dalet*. **Circle** the verb roots, naming each letter as you circle them. **Add** these words to your List of Vocabulary Words.

✡ **Make flash cards** for these verbs. Note: If you have acquired a Hebrew-English Interlinear Old Testament, can you find many places where the "dah-bahr" verb דבר (speak, spoke) is used?

WEEKS 23-24

✡ **Recite** the alef-bet. Always practice for speed and accuracy.

✡ **Fill in** the bottom of the Practice Pages for *lamed* and *mem*, pp. 78, 79.

✡ **Study the pictures** for *lamed*, p. 25.

✡ **Draw** your own pictures for at least two of the words. **Label** and **add** to your abecedary file.

✡ **See "Alef-bet of Verbs,"** p. 62. **Learn** the verb that begins with *hay*. **Circle** the root word in the examples. **Write the verb** in your List of Vocabulary Words to memorize.

✡ **Make a flash card** for this verb.

✡ **Read** the section for the "vahv conversives" on p. 62. Note: There are very few verbs that start with a vahv, so we are giving you examples of "vahv conversives." Read and study them thoroughly. Find other examples of vahv conversives in your Interlinear Bible. Remember that vahv means "and" when attached before a verb or noun.

✡ **Review and recite** verse Isaiah 6:3, page 103.

WEEKS 25-26

✡ **Recite** the alef-bet. Practice **writing** it as well.

✡ **Fill in** the **bottom** half of the Practice Pages for *nun* and *samek*, pp. 80, 81.

✡ **Take Quiz 3** (fill in the blanks), p. 100 in pencil. **Make a copy** and take the quiz the **first** time on the copy. Take Quiz 3 again in week 30.

✡ **Study the pictures** for the *mem* page, p. 27.

✡ **Draw** your own pictures for at least two of the words that begin with *mem*. **Label** and **add** to your own growing abecedary file.

✡ **See "Alef-bet of Verbs,"** p. 63. **Learn** the verbs that begin with *zayin* and *khet*.

✡ **Circle** the verb roots in the sentence examples. **Add** these new verbs to your List of Vocabulary Words, and **make flash cards**.

✡ **Learn to count** from zero to ten. See "Numbers," p. 104.

✡ **NOTE: To any who are not making an "abecedary" with pictures (this might include a parent or older child), you need to AT LEAST make a chart with a memorized word next to each corresponding letter of the Hebrew alef-bet! This would be optional for all those making an abecedary. Hang the chart on the wall for easy viewing and review.**

LESSON PLANS—WEEKS 27-28 (Shade in the Star of David when you finish each assignment.)

✡ **Recite** the Hebrew alef-bet.
✡ **Fill in** the **bottom** of the Practice Pages for *ayin* and *pay/fay,* pp. 82, 83.
✡ **Take Matching Quiz 3,** p. 94 , in pencil. Be sure to read aloud the Hebrew words.
✡ **Study** the pictures on the *nun* page, p. 29.
✡ **Create** your own pictures for *nun* words. **Label** and **add** to the picture abecedary file.
✡ **See "Alef-bet of Verbs,"** p. 63. **Read** examples for *tet* and *yud.* **Circle** the verb roots.
✡ **Learn** the *tet* and *yud* verbs. **Add** to the List of Vocabulary Words, and **make flash cards.**
✡ **Learn to count** from eleven to twenty. See "Numbers," page 104.

WEEKS 29-30

✡ **Recite** the alef-bet. **Play** "Scramble" with the flash cards.
✡ **Fill in** the bottom of the Practice Pages for *tsadee* and *kuf,* pp. 84, 85.
✡ **Take Quiz 3** (fill in the blank) the second time in the book, p. 100. Try not to look up answers this time.
✡ **Study picture words** on the *samek* page, p. 31. Sound out the Hebrew words.
✡ **Create** your own pictures for at least two *samek* words. **Label** and **add** to your abecedary file.
✡ **See "Alef-bet of Verbs,"** pp. 63, 64. **Read** carefully for *kaf* and *lamed.* **Circle** the verb roots in each example.
✡ **Learn to count** from 21 to 30. See page 104.

WEEKS 31-32

✡ **Recite** the Hebrew alef-bet every day.
✡ **Fill in** the bottom of the Practice Pages for *reysh* (week 31), and *seen/sheen* (week 32), pp. 86, 87.
✡ **Make a copy** of Quiz 4 on page 101. **Take Quiz 4** the first time, looking up answers earlier in the book when needed. Take quiz in the book later, week 34.
✡ **Study the picture words** for *ayin* on page 33.
✡ **Create** your own drawings for at least two of these *ayin* words, **label** and **add** them into your abecedary.
✡ **Read and study** the verbs for *mem* and *nun* on page 64, over the next two weeks.
✡ **Learn** the verbs and **add** to your List of Vocabulary Words. **Circle** the verb roots on these pages. **Make flash cards** of the verbs.
✡ **Learn to say** Bible Memory Verse, p. 103 for Week 31. Psalm 119:18. It is not necessary at this time to be able to write it in Hebrew. Just learn to **say** it, as well as **read** it in Hebrew.
✡ **Review** counting from zero to 30. See page 104.

WEEKS 33-34

✡ **Recite** the alef-bet every day! Can you recite within 15 seconds? Play "Scramble" game.
✡ **Fill in** bottom of Practice Page for *tahv,* p. 88.
✡ **Take Quiz 4,** p. 101, the second time.
✡ **Study** the pictures for *pay/fay* on page 35.
✡ **Create** new pictures for at least two of these words. **Label** with Hebrew words and **add** to your file.
(See the next page to continue weeks 33-34.)

✡ **Study** "Alef-bet of Verbs" for *samek* and *ayin*, p. 64. Circle the 3 letters in the verb roots.

✡ **Learn** these verbs, **making flash cards**.

✡ **Review and recite** the verse Psalm 119:18. See page 103.

✡ **Learn to count** by tens up to one hundred. See "Numbers," page 104.

✡ **Read** "How to Use James Strong's *Exhaustive Concordance of the Bible*," p. 108; follow the instructions.

✡ **Do** the "Strong's Assignment," No. 1, on p. 109. Follow all instructions.

WEEKS 35-36

✡ **Recite** the alef-bet every day. Play "Scramble" game.

✡ **Study** the word pictures for *tsadee* on page 37. Sound out the words.

✡ **Create** at least two new pictures for *tsadee*. **Label** and **add** to the abecedary file.

✡ **Make a copy** of Quiz 5 on page 102. **Take this quiz** the first time. You may look up answers from the pictures in the front of the book. Take quiz again in Week 37.

✡ **Read and study** the examples for *pay/fay* and *tsadee* on "Alef-bet of Verbs," p. 65. Circle the three-letter verb roots in the examples. **Make flash cards** of these verbs.

✡ **Learn** the list of pronouns on page 106: I, you, he, she, it, we, you, they.

✡ **Follow instructions** for "Strong's Assignment" No. 2, on page 109.

✡ **Follow directions** for No. 3 on page 109.

✡ **Follow instructions** for No. 4 and No. 5 on page 109.

WEEKS 37-38

✡ **Recite** the alef-bet every day.

✡ **Study the pictures** on *kuf* and *reysh* pages, pp. 39, 41. Sound out the words.

✡ **Create** pictures of your own that begin with *kuf* and *reysh*. **Label** and **add** to the abecedary file.

✡ **Take Quiz 5** on p. 102 for the second time.

✡ **Take Matching Quiz 4**, p. 95, in pencil. Read the Hebrew aloud.

✡ **See "Alef-bet of Verbs,"** pp. 65, 66. **Read** the examples for *kuf* and *reysh*. Sound out the verbs. Circle the verb roots. **Add** the words to your List of Vocabulary Words and **make flash cards**.

✡ **Sound out** the words on the "Names" page, p. 97. **Write** the names in **English**.

✡ **Review** Counting.

✡ **Complete exercise** No. 6 of "Strong's Assignment," on page 110.

WEEKS 39-40

✡ **Recite** the alef-bet every day. **Time** how long it takes you to recite the entire alef-bet accurately.

✡ **Study** the words on the picture pages for *sheen* and *tahv*, pp. 43, 45.

✡ **Draw** your own new pictures for *sheen* and *tahv*. **Label** and **add** to your abecedary file.

✡ **Take Matching Quiz 5**, p. 96, reading the Hebrew aloud.

✡ **See "Alef-bet of Verbs,"** p. 66. Read examples for *sheen* and *tahv*. Sound out the verbs. Circle the verb roots. **Add** the words to your list of Vocabulary Words. **Make flash cards.**

✡ **Complete** exercises 7 to 10 of "Strong's Assignment," p. 110.

✡ **Staple or tie** all the pages of your own creations together and **make a cover** for your abecedary.

✡ **Enjoy your creation and Read/Review often!**

PURPOSE OF THIS BOOK

The purpose behind the making of this book is, very simply, to learn to read in the Hebrew language.

By a careful study of the material, the student will learn the Hebrew letters and vowels, and the sounds they make, until he/she is putting several syllables together to form words, much as a child begins to read in English, for example. He/she will also begin to build a valuable vocabulary.

A good share of the examples is based upon words found in the Tanach, or Old Testament, so this book should be of special interest to those who love God's Word and would desire to know it better, to the glory of God.

Hebrew: Beginning Your Journey is written for all ages, but is especially geared to the older student or home school parent, who would also learn and be able to guide the younger ones in the family. This book by itself can be used to learn basic Hebrew, but the beginner is encouraged to take advantage of other sources as well.

Depending on the age of the student and his/her aggressiveness, the mastering of the material in this book may be spread out over a year or less. It is recommended that this material be divided into individual lessons over the course of forty weeks. **Be sure to see the section on "LESSON PLANS FOR THE YEAR: HOW TO USE THIS BOOK," pp. C-I. Begin there!**

It is hoped that as the student begins to understand Hebrew, he/she will have the appetite whetted to continue searching the Old Testament's original Hebrew, as for "hidden treasure," long after he/she has mastered the things herein.

ASIA MINOR

Haran.

Cyprus

Mediterranean   Sea

Sidon.

Damascus

Tyre.
Mt. Hermon

Mt. Carmel
Sea of Galilee

Jordan

Tel Aviv
Jericho
Jerusalem
Bethlehem
Dead Sea
ISRAEL

Alexandria

EGYPT

*Cairo

Petra.

SINAI
PENINSULA

ARABIA

Mt. Sinai?

Turn to Me and be saved, all the ends of the earth (אָרֶץ); for I am God, and none else (is). Isaiah 45:22

Alef is for...

אֱלֹהִים
(Elo-HEEM)
God

אַבָּא
(AH-bah)
father, dad

אִמָּא
(EE-mah)
mother

אָדָם
(ah-DAHM)
man

אֲבִיגַיִל
Abigail

אַבְרָהָם
Abraham

אָדָם
Adam

אַהֲרוֹן
Aaron

אֵלִיָּהוּ
Elijah

אֱלִישֶׁבַע
Elizabeth

אָשֵׁר
Asher

אֶרֶץ
(AH-rets)
earth

אֳנִיָּה
(oh-nee-YAH)
ship

1

אֶחָד
(eh-KHAHD)
one

אוֹר
(ore)
light

(He is)
eating (oh-KHEL) אֹכֵל

Hear, O Israel: the LORD our God, (אֱלֹהֵינוּ) the LORD is one (אֶחָד). Deuteronomy 6:4 NKJV™

And Israel stretched out his right hand, and laid it upon Ephraim's head, who was the younger, and his left hand upon Manasseh's head, guiding his hands wittingly; for Manasseh was the firstborn... And he blessed them (וַיְבָרֶךְ) that day, saying, 'In thee shall Israel bless, (יְבָרֵךְ) saying, God make thee as Ephraim and as Manasseh; and he set Ephraim before Manasseh.' Genesis 48:14, 20 KJV

4

Bet is for...

בְּרָכָה
(b'-rah-KHAH)
blessing

house
בֵּית
(BAH-yeet)

בָּנִים
(bah-NEEM)
sons

בָּנוֹת
(bah-NOTE)
daughters

בָּבֶל
Babel (Babylon)

בַּת-שֶׁבַע
Bath-sheba

בֵּלְטְשַׁאצַּר
Belteshazzar (Daniel)

בִּנְיָמִין
Benjamin

בֵּית-אֵל
Bethel

בְּעוּלָה
Beulah

בֹּעַז
Boaz

בֶּרֶךְ
(BEH-rech)
knee

בָּצָל
(bah-TSAHL)
onion

בָּרָק
(bah-RAHK)
lightning

בּוֹרֵא
(boh-RAY)
create

בְּהֵמוֹת
(b'-HAY-mote)
behemoth / beast

In the beginning God created (בָּרָא) the heavens and the earth. Genesis 1:1 NKJV™

5

And when she had finished giving him a drink, she said, "I will draw water for your camels (לִגְמַלֶּיךָ) also, until they have finished drinking." Genesis 24:19 NKJV™

6

Gimel is for...

גִּבּוֹר
(gee-BOHR)
mighty, strong one, hero

גְּבִנָה
(g'-vee-NAH)
cheese

גֶּפֶן
(GEH-fen)
grapevine

גֶּשֶׁם
(GEH-shem)
rain

ג׳יֽרָפָה
(jee-RAH-fah*)
giraffe

*This "foreign" word begins with a "g" that is an *exception* in Hebrew, sounding as "g" in "gel."

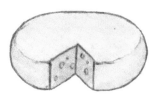

גַּבְרִיאֵל
Gabriel

גָּד
Gad

גִּדְעוֹן
Gideon

גָּלְיָת
Goliath

גִּלְעָד
Gilead

גֹּשֶׁן
Goshen

גְּדִי
(g'-DEE)
kid, baby goat

גָּמָל
(gah-MAHL)
camel

גַּלְגַּל
(gahl-gahl)
wheel

garden   (gahn)   גַּן

And David (דָּוִד) behaved himself wisely in all his ways; and the LORD was with him. I Samuel 18:14 KJV

Dalet is for... דֶּרֶךְ

(DEH-rekh)
way

דָּג
(dahg)
fish

דֶּגֶל
(DEH-gehl)
flag

דֶּלֶת
(DEH-let)
door

דָּוִד
(Dah-VEED)
David

(David and Goliath)

דְּבוֹרָה
Deborah

דָּוִד
David

דְּלִילָה
Delilah

דָּן
Dan

דָּנִיֵּאל
Daniel

דֹּתָן
Dothan

דְּבוֹרָה
(devo-RAH)
bee

דּוֹד
(dōhd)
uncle

דּוֹדָה
(doh-DAH)
aunt

bear   (dōhv)   דּוֹב

Teach me, O LORD, the way (דֶּרֶךְ) of Thy statutes, and I will keep it unto the end. Psalm 119:33 KJV

9

Bryce Canyon, Utah

I will muse on the glorious honor (הָדָר) of Your majesty and the things of your wonderful works. Psalm 145:5

Marion Merritt

Hay is for... הָדָר and הוֹד

(hah-DAR)
glorious, majestic

(hohd)
honorable, majestic

הוֹרִים
(ho-REEM)
parents

Mt. Sinai

הַר
(hahr)
mountain

הֵיכָל
(hay-KHAL)
palace
(biblical usage)

הֶבֶל
Abel

הָגָר
Hagar

הִלֵּל
Hillel

הָרָן
Haran

הַשֵׁם
Hashem
(the Name of the Lord)

הַס
(hahs)
Hush!
Be silent!

הֲדַסָּה
(hah-dah-SAH)
Hadassah
(Esther)

הַ (ha), when prefixed
to a word, means "the."

הַכִּיסֵא
(ha-KEE-say)
the chair

הַלְלוּ
(hah-LAY-loo)
Hallelu/Praise
"Praise Him with the sound
of the trumpet." Psalm 150:3

The Infant Samuel by Sir Joshua Reynolds

(heet-pah-LALE)
he prayed
הִתְפַּלֵּל

His work is honorable and glorious; (הוֹד־וְהָדָר) and His righteousness endures forever. Psalm 111:3 NKJV™

11

...And God said, let the earth sprout tender sprouts, the plant seeding seed, the fruit tree producing fruit according to its kind, whichever seed is in it on the earth. And it was so. (וַיְהִי-כֵן) Gen. 1:11

12

Vahv is for...

וָו
(vahv)
hook

Vahv, when prefixed to a word, is the conjunction "and." God is as the "hook" who brings men to Himself.

"And God called **(וַיִּקְרָא אֱלֹהִים)** the light Day." Genesis 1:5
(vah- yee-KRAH Elo-HEEM)

"And God created **(וַיִּבְרָא אֱלֹהִים)** the man in His own image." Genesis 1:27
(vah-yee-VRAH Elo-HEEM)

"And the LORD God said, **(וַיֹּאמֶר יְהֹוָה אֱלֹהִים)**
(vah-yo-MEHR Adonai Elo-HEEM)
It is not good that man should be alone. I will make him a helper comparable to him." Genesis 2:18 NKJV™

"And God saw **(וַיַּרְא אֱלֹהִים)** everything that He had made, and, behold, it was very good!" Genesis 1:31
(vah-YAHR Elo-HEEM)

"And God remembered **(וַיִּזְכֹּר אֱלֹהִים)**
(vah-yeez-KORE Elo-HEEM)
Noah, and every living thing, and all the cattle which were with him in the ark. And God made a wind to pass over the earth, and the waters subsided." Gensis 8:1

"And God blessed **(וַיְבָרֶךְ אֱלֹהִים)** the seventh day and sanctified it." Genesis 2:3
(vah-y'-vah-REKH Elo-HEEM)

But when the fulness of the time was come, God sent forth His Son, made of a woman, made under the law, to redeem them that were under the law... Galatians 4:4 KJV. Behold, the virgin shall conceive and bear a Son, and shall call His name Immanuel. Isaiah 7:14 NKJV™

זַמְּרוּ אֱלֹהִים זַמֵּרוּ זַמְּרוּ לְמַלְכֵּנוּ זַמֵּרוּ   Psalm 47:6

Pronounced as: (Zahm-ROO Elo-HEEM, zah-MAY-roo; zahm-ROO l'-mal-KAY-noo, zah-MAY-roo.)

Sing praise (זַמְּרוּ) to God, sing praise (זַמְּרוּ); Sing praise (זַמְּרוּ) to our king, sing praise (זַמְּרוּ).   Psalm 47:6

 # Zayin is for... זֶרַע

(ZEH-rah)

seed

זָקָן
(zah-KAHN)
beard

זֵיתִים
(zay-TEEM)
olives

זְבֻלוּן
Zebulon

זְכַרְיָהוּ
Zachariah

זִלְפָּה
Zilpah

זַחַל
(zah-KHAL)
caterpillar

זָהָב
(zah-HAHV)
gold

זֶבְרָה
(zeb-RAH)
zebra

זְאֵב
(z'-EHV)
wolf

And I will put enmity between you and the woman, and between your seed (זַרְעֲךָ)
and her seed (זַרְעָהּ). He will bruise your head, and you shall bruise his heel. Genesis 3:15

The Angel of the LORD encamps (חָנָה) [pitches a tent] all around those who fear Him, and delivers them. Psalm 34:7 NKJV™

 Khet is for...

חַנּוּן
(khah-NOON)
gracious

See the bottom of p. 48 for the pronunciation of the "kh" in "Khet" words.

חֲבֵרִים
(khah-vay-REEM)
friends

חָתוּל
(khah-TOOL)
cat

חָמֵשׁ
(khah-MAYSH)
five

חֶבְרוֹן
Hebron

חִדֶּקֶל
Hiddekell (Tigris)

חַנָּה
Hannah

חַוָּה
Eve

חוּר
Hur

חִזְקִיָּה
Hezekiah

חִלְקִיָּהוּ
Hilkiah

חֹרֵב
Horeb

חֶרֶב
(KHEH-rehv)
sword

חֵץ
(khayts)
arrow

חַלּוֹן
(khah-LONE)
window

חָלָב
(kha-LAHV)
milk

beetle

חִיפוּשִׁית
(khee-poo-SHEET)

...For You are a gracious (חַנּוּן) and merciful God. Nehemiah 9:31

17

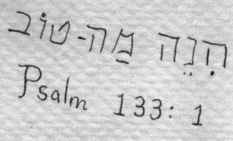

הִנֵּה מַה־טּוֹב
Psalm 133: 1

הִנֵּה מַה־טּוֹב וּ־מַה־נָּ־עִים

He - nay mah tov oo - ma nah - eem

Be - hold! How good and how plea - sant

שֶׁבֶת אַ־חִים גַּם יַ־חַד

sheh - vet ah - kheem, gam yah - khad!

(is the) living (of) brothers, even (in) unity!

18

טַיָּס
(tah-YAHS)
pilot

טַבָּעוֹת
(tah-bah-OHT)
rings

בּוֹקֶר טוֹב
(BO-kehr tohv)
Good morning!

יוֹם טוֹב
(yohm tohv)
Good day!

עֶרֶב טוֹב
(EH-rev tohv)
Good evening!

טַלִּית
(tah-LEET)
prayer shawl

טַבָּח
(tah-BACH)
chef

טַיּוֹן
(tay-OHN)
teapot

טַוָּס
(tah-VAHS)
peacock

Oh, give thanks to the LORD, for He is good! (טוֹב) For His mercy endures forever. Psalm 136:1 NKJV™

Whatever your hand (יָדְךָ) finds to do, do it with your might. Ecclesiastes 9:10

Yud is for...

יָד
(yahd)
hand

יְרוּשָׁלַיִם Jerusalem

יָרֵחַ
(yah-RAY-ahch)
moon

יַלְדָּה
(Yahl-DAH)
girl

יוֹאֵל
Joel

יוֹנָה
Jonah

יוֹנָתָן
Jonathan

יוֹסֵף
Joseph

יַעֲקֹב
Jacob

יִצְחָק
Isaac

יְרִיחוֹ
Jericho

יִרְמְיָהוּ
Jeremiah

יֵשׁוּעַ
Yeshua (Jesus)

יֶלֶד
(YEH-led)
boy

יַהֲלֹם
(yah-ha-LOHM)
diamond

יֶרֶק
(YEH-rehk)
vegetable

יָעֵן
(yah-AYN)
ostrich

יַעַר
(yah-AHR)
forest

יוֹנָה
(yoh-NAH)
dove

יַרְדֵּן Jordan (River)

And he [manslayer] shall live in that city until he stands before the congregation for judgment, until the death of the high priest (הַכֹּהֵן הַגָּדוֹל) who is in those days. Joshua 20:6

Kaf is for...

כָּבוֹד
(kah-VOHD)
glory

כֶּתֶר
(KEH-tehr)
crown

כֶּבֶשׂ
(KEH-vehs)
sheep

כַּף מְצִלְתַּיִם
(kaf meh-tseel-ta-YEEM)
cymbals

כּוֹתֶל
(KO-tel)
Western wall

כַּרְמֶל
Carmel

כּוֹכָבִים
(ko-khah-VEEM)
stars

(יוֹם) כִּפּוּר
(Yom) Kippur,
(Day of Atonement)

כֶּלֶב
(KEH-lehv)
dog

כַּלָּה
(kah-LAH)
bride

violin כִּנּוֹר
(kee-NOHR)

The heavens proclaim the glory (כָּבוֹד) of God. Psalm 19:1

And you, Bethlehem (בֵּית־לֶחֶם) Ephratah, you who are little among the thousands of Judah, out of you He shall come forth to Me to be ruler in Israel, and His goings forth (have been) from of old, from the days of eternity. Micah 5:2

בֵּית לֶחֶם
Bethlehem
(House of Bread)

24

 # Lamed is for... לֶחֶם

(LEH-khem)
bread

לְוִיָתָן
(leev-yah-TAHN)
whale/leviathan

לְבִיאָה
(l'-VEE-ah)
lioness

לִמוֹן
(lee-MOHN)
lemon

לֵאָה
Leah

לָבָן
Laban

לֵוִי
Levi

לַיְלָה טוֹב
Good night!

לוֹטוּס
(loh-TOOS)
lotus/water lily

לַיְלָה
(LIE-lah)
night

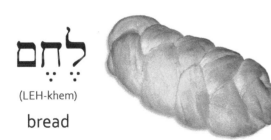
לֶחֶם
(LEH-khem)
bread

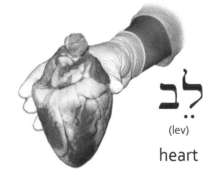
לֵב
(lev)
heart

Even my friend...who ate of my bread (לַחְמִי), has lifted up his heel against me. Psalm 41:9

25

The king's heart (לֶב־מֶלֶךְ) (is) in the hand of the LORD, (like) the rivers of water; He turns it wherever He wishes. Proverbs 21:1 NKJV™

מִצְוָה
(MITZ-vah)
commandment,
good deed

מֵנָה
אַחֲרוֹנָה
(mah-NAH akh-ro-NAH,
lit. - mahna, "course",
akhronah, "last")

dessert

מֶלֶךְ
(MEH-lehkh)
king

מִיכָאֵל
Michael

מִרְיָם
Miriam

מָרְדְּכַי
Mordecai

מֹרִיָּה
Moriah

מִצְרַיִם
Egypt

מֹשֶׁה
Moses

מָשִׁיחַ
Messiah

מְתוּשֶׁלַח
Methusaleh

מַלְאָכִי
Malachi

מַצָּה
(MAH-tsah)
matzah

מֶרְכָּבָה
(mehr-KAH-vah)
chariot

מְנוֹרָה
(meh-NO-rah)
menorah

מִזְרָקָה
(meez-RAH-kah)
fountain

key   (maf-tay-AKH)   מַפְתֵּחַ

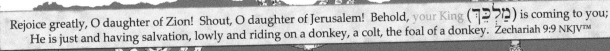

Rejoice greatly, O daughter of Zion! Shout, O daughter of Jerusalem! Behold, your King (מֶלֶךְ) is coming to you;
He is just and having salvation, lowly and riding on a donkey, a colt, the foal of a donkey. Zechariah 9:9 NKJV™

27

"Praise Him with the psaltery and harp (בְּנֵבֶל)." Psalm 150:3b KJV

Nun is for...

נֵר
(nayr)
candle, lamp
(biblical usage)

נְמָלָה
(n'-MAH-lah)
ant

candle   (nayr)   נֵר

נוֹצָה
(no-TSAH)
feather

נֵבֶל
(NEH-vehl)
harp

נְבוֹ
Nebo

נֶגֶב
Negev

נֹחַ
Noah

נִינְוֵה
Ninevah

נָעֳמִי
Naomi

נַפְתָּלִי
Naphtali

נְתַנְאֵל
Nathaniel

נָהָר
(nah-HAHR)
river

נֶשֶׁר
(NEH-shehr)
eagle

נָחָשׁ
(nah-KHASH)
serpent, snake

(nah-MAYR)   נָמֵר
tiger

For Thou art my lamp (נֵרִי), O LORD: and the LORD will lighten my darkness. 2 Samuel 22:29 KJV

Then the disciples took him by night and let him down through the wall in a large basket (סַל). Acts 9:25 NKJV™

Samek is for...

סֵפֶר
(SAY-fehr)
book

סֵפֶל
(SAY-fel)
cup

סֵפֶר
(SAY-fehr)
book

סַל
(sahl)
basket

סוֹפֵר
(soh-FAYR)
scribe

סְדֹם
Sodom

סוּכּוֹת
Sukkot

סִינַי
Sinai

סֶלַע
Sela

סוּס
(soos)
horse

סוּסוֹן יָם
(soo-sohn YAHM)
seahorse

סְבִיבוֹן
(s'-vee-VOHN)
dreidal

salad   (sahl-AHT)   סָלָט

Then the LORD appeared to him [Abraham] by the terebinth trees of Mamre,...and behold, three men were standing by him; and when he saw them, he ran from the tent door to meet them, and bowed himself to the ground, and said,... "Please let a little water be brought, and wash your feet, and rest yourselves under the tree (הָעֵץ)." Genesis 18:1,2,4 NKJV™

עַיִן
(AH-yeen)
eye

tree (aytz) עֵץ

עֻגָה
(oo-GAH)
cake

עַכְבָּר
(akh-BAHR)
mouse

עִמָּנוּאֵל
Immanuel ("With us, God")

עֵדֶן
Eden

עֵין־גֶּדִי
Engedi

עֵלִי
Eli

עָמוֹס
Amos

עִבְרִי
Hebrew

עֲנָקִים
Anakim (giants)

עֶצֶם
(EH -tsem)
bone

עַגְבָנִיָּה
(ahg-vah-nee-YAH)
tomato

עוּגָב
(oo-GAHV)
organ

עֲטַלֵּף
(ah-tah-LAYF)
bat

eyes עֵינַיִם
(ay-NAH-yeem)

The eyes (עֵינֵי) of the LORD are in every place, beholding the evil and the good. Prov. 15:3 KJV

My God, My God, why have You forsaken Me? Why are You so far from helping Me, and from the words of My roaring? Many bulls have compassed Me: strong bulls of Bashan have beset Me round... They gaped upon Me with their mouths (פִּיהֶם), as a ravening and a roaring lion. Psalm 22:1,12,13 KJV

Pay is for...

פֶּה
(peh)
mouth

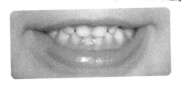

פֶּה
(peh)
mouth

פְּנִינָה
(p'-nee-NAH)
pearl

פַּטִּישׁ
(pah-TEESH)
hammer

פּוּרִים
Purim

פִּישׁוֹן
Pishon (river of Eden)

פֶּלֶג
Peleg

פֶּרַח
(PEH-rach)
flower

פִּסְגָּה
Pisgah

פֶּסַח
Passover

פַּרְעֹה
Pharoah

פְּרָת
Euphrates

פַּרְפַּר
(pahr-PAHR)
butterfly

פֵּירוֹת
(pay-ROHT)
fruits

פְּסַנְתֵּר
(p'-sahn-TAYR)
piano

elephant   (peel)   פִּיל

...and every animal after its kind, and every creeping thing...after its kind,...and every bird (צִפּוֹר) of every sort;
And they went in to Noah and to the ark, two and two of all flesh, in which (is) the breath of life. Genesis 7:14,15

צְנוֹנִית
(ts'-no-NEET)

radish

צַפְצָפָה *
(tsaf-tsah-FAH)

willow tree
*As found in Ezekiel 17:5.

צְפַרְדֵּעַ
(ts'-far-DAY-ah)

frog

צַלָּם
(tsah-LAHM)

photographer

צִדְקִיָּהוּ
Zedekiah

צִיּוֹן
Zion

צְפַנְיָה
Zephaniah

צִפֹּרָה
Zipporah

צָעִיף
(tsa-EEF)

scarf, veil

צָב
(tsahv)

turtle
(or tortoise)

צִפּוֹר
(tsee-POR)

bird

bracelet   (tsah-MEED)

צָמִיד

The LORD is righteous (צַדִּיק) in all His ways, and holy in all His works. Psalm 145:17 NKJV™

And God spoke to Noah, and to his sons with him, saying, ..."When I gather clouds on the earth, then the bow (קֶשֶׁת) shall be seen in the clouds, and I will remember My covenant which is between Me and you and every living soul in all flesh; and the waters shall not again become a flood to destroy all flesh." Genesis 9:8,14,15

38

Kuf is for...

(ka-DOHSH)
holy

nest (kane) קֵן

קוֹנְכִיָּה
(kohn-kee-YAH)
shell

קַיְוִי
(KEE-vee)
kiwi

קַיִן
Cain

קִישׁ
Kish

קֶשֶׁת
בֶּעָנָן
(KEH-shet
b'-ah-NAHN)
rainbow

קִדְרוֹן
Kidron (valley)

קוֹף
(kohf)
monkey

קָדֵשׁ־בַּרְנֵעַ
Kadesh-Barnea

קְטוּרָה
Keturah

קִנָּמוֹן
(kee-nah-MOHN)
cinnamon

קַדָּר
(kah-DAHR)
potter

קְלַרְנִית
clarinet (klahr'-NEET)

Holy, holy, holy (קָדוֹשׁ) is the LORD of hosts; the whole earth is full of His glory. Isaiah 6:3 KJV

39

As a shepherd (רָעָה) seeks his flock..., so I will seek out My sheep, and will deliver them from all the places where they were scattered. Ezekiel 34:12

Reysh is for...

רֹאשׁ
(rohsh)
head

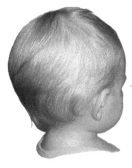

רֹאשׁ
(rohsh)
head

רוֹעֶה
(roh-EH)
shepherd

רִיבָּה
(ree-BAH)
jam

רְאוּבֵן
Reuben

רִבְקָה
Rebekah

רָחָב
Rahab

רוּת
Ruth

רְחַבְעָם
Rehoboam

רָחֵל
Rachael

רְפָאֵל
Raphael

רוּחַ הַקֹּדֶשׁ
Holy Spirit

רָקוּן
(rah-KOON)
raccoon

רוּחַ
(roo-AHCH)
wind

רוֹפֵא
(roh-FAY)
doctor

רֶגֶל
(REH-gel)
foot

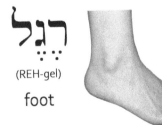

רִימוֹן
(ree-MOHN)
pomegranate

Damascus Gate

Lift up your heads, O gates (שְׁעָרִים); and be lifted up, O everlasting doors,
and the King of glory shall come in. Psalm 24:7

Eastern Gate

42

Sheen is for...

שָׁלוֹם
(shalom)
peace

שָׁעוֹן
(shah-OHN)
watch

שֶׁמֶשׁ
(SHEH-mesh)
sun

שׁוֹפָר
(shoh-FAHR)
shofar, trumpet,
(biblical usage)

שַׁבָּת
Sabbath

שִׁילֹה
Shiloh

שְׁלֹמֹה
Solomon

שְׁמוּאֵל
Samuel

שִׁמְשׁוֹן
Samson

שָׁרוֹן
Sharon

שׁוּם
(shoom)
garlic

שׁוֹשַׁנָּה
(shoh-shah-NAH)
rose

שַׁעַר
(shah-AHR)
gate

7

(sheev-AH)
seven

שִׁבְעָה

שׁוֹרֶשׁ
(sho-RESH)
root

The LORD will give strength unto his people; the LORD will bless his people with peace (בְּשָׁלוֹם). Psalm 29:11 KJV

Ha-Tikva

Kol od ba-le-vav pe-ni-ma, ... e-fesh Ye-hu-di ... a... ...na, ...ti... tik-va te... bat shnot al-pa-yim li-heyot am ch... tze-nu e-retz Tzi-yon vi-...sha-la-yim. Li-heyot am chof-shi be-ar...tze-nu e-retz Tzi-yon vi-Y'ru-sha-la-yim.

Tahv is for...

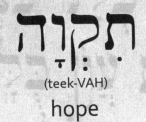

תִּקְוָה
(teek-VAH)
hope

תַּרְנְגוֹל
(tahr-n'-GOHL)
rooster

תֵּשַׁע
(TAY-shah)
nine

תֻּכִּי
(TOO-kee)
parrot

תַּפּוּז
(tah-POOZ)
orange

תָּבוֹר
Tabor

תּוֹרָה
Torah (Law of Moses)

תֵּל אָבִיב
Tel-aviv

תָּמָר
Tamar

תֶּרַח
Terah

תַּרְשִׁישׁ
Tarshish

תַּפּוּחַ
(tah-poo-AHKH)
apple

תַּנִּין
(tah-NEEN)
crocodile

תִּירָס
(tee-RAHS)
corn

palm (tree)
(ayts tah-MAHR)
(עֵץ) תָּמָר

א בב ג ד ה ו

alef   vet / bet   gimel   dalet   hay   vahv

ז ח ט י כ כ ל

zayin   khet   tet   yud   khaf / kaf   lamed

מ נ ס ע פ פ

mem   nun   samek   ayin   fay / pay

צ ק ר שׁ שׁ ת

tsadee   kuf   reysh   seen / sheen   tahv

✡

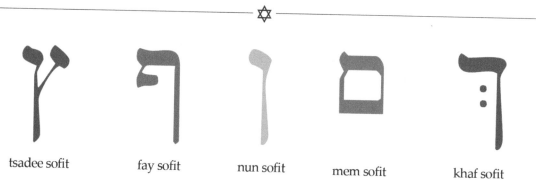

ך ם ן ף ץ

khaf sofit   mem sofit   nun sofit   fay sofit   tsadee sofit

46

WATCH THE "LOOK-ALIKES"!

Many of the Hebrew letters look very much alike. Study these and learn the differences between them. For instance, the only difference between the "hay" (ה) and "khet" (ח) is that the "hay" is open on the left side and the "khet" is closed.

Here are some look-alikes:

ד (dalet, d)	ך (final khaf, kh)	כ (kaf, k)	ב (bet, b)
ס (samek, s)	ם (final mem, m)	ף (final fay, f)	ך (final khaf, kh)
ד (dalet, d)	ר (reysh, r)	ת (tahv, t)	ה (hay, h)
ע (ayin, silent)	צ (tsadee, ts)	ו (vahv, v)	ר (reysh, r)
ו (vahv, v)	ן (nun, n)	ב (vet, v)	כ (khaf, kh)
ו (vahv, v)	ז (zayin, z)	י (yud, y)	ו (vahv, v)
ת (tahv, t)	ח (khet, kh)	ו (vahv, v)	ן (final nun, n)
שׂ (seen, s)	שׁ (sheen, sh)	ז (zayin, z)	ן (final nun, n)
ג (gimel, g)	נ (nun, n)	ץ (final tsadee, ts)	ע (ayin, silent)
ט (tet, t)	מ (mem, m)	ה (hay, h)	ח (khet, kh)
כ (khaf, kh)	ב (vet, v)		

47

PRONUNCIATION GUIDE

Throughout the book you will find helps in how to pronounce the Hebrew letters and vowel sounds.

✡ On each Picture Page you will find the pronunciation of Hebrew words in parentheses.

✡ Each time a syllable in parentheses is CAPITALIZED, that is the syllable to be accented heavier.

✡ You will notice that the majority of times, the LAST syllable of the Hebrew words is accented the heaviest.

✡ Try to "roll the Rs" slightly.

✡ See NIKOOD, page 49, for explanation of vowel sounds.

✡ Study all the "Notes on the Hebrew Alef-bet," pages 55-60, for letter sounds.

✡ Reading Practice Pages 89-91 will show how consonants and vowels sound together.

✡ "AH" when in pronunciation parentheses is always an "ah" like in "father."
For example, on the א (alef) picture page, p. 3, you will see six pictured words which have the "AH" sound. Look for the AH, for example, in the word like "one,"(eh-KHAHD).

✡ "OH" = the "o" sound as in "boat," a long "o" sound.
"OO" = "oo" as in "boot."

✡ You will see the guttural sounds for ך (khaf sofit), כ (khaf), and ח (khet), spelled with a "kh." Be sure to always pronounce them with the extra airy, guttural sound, as we would say the "ch" in Johann Sebastian Bach's name. The gutteral sound may also be compared to the "ch" in the Scottish word "loch." Note: Some other study books may spell these letters as chaf and chet (with a ch), but either way, it is the same sound.

HEBREW VOWEL SYSTEM (NIKOOD)

Here are the symbols of the Hebrew vowels. Most will appear under a letter. The consonant letter above them is pronounced first, and then the vowel sound under. See Examples below.

- **:**   Shva - a shortened, quickened, slurred letter sound

- **ָ**   Kamatz - "ah" as in *father*;   **ָ:** khataf kamatz - sounds like "oh."

- **ַ**   Patakh - "ah" as in *father*;   **ֲ** khataf patach also sounds like "ah."

- **ֶ**   Segol - "eh" as in *head*;   **ֱ** khataf segol also sounds like "eh."

- **ֵ**   Tzayray - "ay" as in *say*; הֵ = "hay"; בֵּ = "bay"; דֵ = "day"; סֵ = "say," etc.

- **ִ**   Kheereek - with or without the yud - "ee," as in *see*

- **ֹ**   Kholam - "oh" as in *go*. The dot appears *above* and to the *left* of the letter.

- **ֹו**   Kholam with vahv - "oh" as in *go*

- **וּ**   Shoorook with vahv - "oo" as in *spoon*

- **ֻ**   Koobootz - "oo" as in *spoon*. This appears **under** the letter.

It is good for the older beginner to learn the names of these vowel symbols. However, it is MORE important to know the sounds the vowel symbols stand for and how they sound in combination with the consonant letter.

For example: the Patakh.   אַ = "ah,"   בַּ = "bah,"   לַ = "lah,"   מַ = "mah,"   גַ = "gah," etc.

Examples

Shva - בְּרֵאשִׁית "B'-ray-SHEET," "In the beginning"...

Kamatz - סָלָט "sah-LAHT";   בָּרָא "bah-RAH"

Patakh - הַר "har";   יַעַר "yah-AHR"

Segol - אֶל "el";   דֶּלֶת "DEH-let"

Tzayray - עֵץ "aytz";   סֵפֶר "SAY-fehr"

Kheereek - גְּדִי "g'-DEE";   אִמָּא "EE-mah"

Kholam - Noah's name in Hebrew is נֹחַ   Notice the dot (kholam) following the nun, to give the "oh" sound; "peace" also has a vahv with kholam: שָׁלוֹם "shah-LOHM"

Shoorook - סוּס "soos";   וּמַה "oo-MAH"

Koobootz - תֻּכִּי "TOO-key";   סֻכּוֹת "soo-KOHT"

> In the early copies of Scriptures there were no vowel markings. They were added to help beginners learn to read. After you know the words, you, too, should no longer need the vowel points to be able to read.

CAN YOU FIND THE "A-B-Cs"?

Here is a great way to practice using your Hebrew A-B-Cs! Did you know there are several chapters in the Old Testament (Tanach) which are written in Hebrew "alphabetical form"? They were divinely laid out so that the verses begin with the letters of the Hebrew alphabet in consecutive order. There are some minor variations in different chapters, i.e., a letter may be repeated or left out, but essentially all are in order. Many feel this was done to help in memorization and to bring closer attention to the passage. Keep in mind that from ancient times it was thought that there lay beneath the text a deeper meaning—that each individual letter had a spiritual import.

Directions: Circle (in pencil) the first letter of each verse. (A colon separates the verses.) The arrow tells you where to begin. When you have circled all of the alphabet letters, ask yourself if there were any letters "out of order," or if there were any letters missing. After completing this exercise, see the answer key on page 112 for additional comments.

Psalm 34

לְדָוִד בְּשַׁנּוֹתוֹ אֶת־טַעְמוֹ לִפְנֵי אֲבִימֶלֶךְ וַיְגָרְשֵׁהוּ וַיֵּלַךְ׃

| | A Psalm of David, | when he changed | his behaviour | before | Abimelech; | who drove him away, | and he departed. |

אֲבָרְכָה אֶת־יְהוָה בְּכָל־עֵת תָּמִיד תְּהִלָּתוֹ בְּפִי׃

1

| | I will bless | the LORD | at all times: | shall continually be | his praise | in my mouth. |

בַּיהוָה תִּתְהַלֵּל נַפְשִׁי יִשְׁמְעוּ עֲנָוִים וְיִשְׂמָחוּ׃ גַּדְּלוּ

2
3

| | in the LORD: | shall make her boast | My soul | shall hear thereof, | the humble | and be glad. | O magnify |

לַיהוָה אִתִּי וּנְרוֹמְמָה שְׁמוֹ יַחְדָּו׃ דָּרַשְׁתִּי אֶת־יְהוָה וְעָנָנִי

3
4

| | the LORD | with me, | and let us exalt | his name | together. | I sought | the LORD, | and he heard me, |

וּמִכָּל־מְגוּרוֹתַי הִצִּילָנִי׃ הִבִּיטוּ אֵלָיו וְנָהָרוּ וּפְנֵיהֶם אַל־יֶחְפָּרוּ׃

4
5

| | and from all | my fears | delivered me. | They looked | unto him, | and were lightened: | and their faces | were not ashamed. |

זֶה עָנִי קָרָא וַיהוָה שָׁמֵעַ וּמִכָּל־צָרוֹתָיו הוֹשִׁיעוֹ׃

6

| | This | poor man | cried, | and the LORD | heard *him*, | and out of all | his troubles | saved him. |

חֹנֶה מַלְאַךְ־יְהוָה סָבִיב לִירֵאָיו וַיְחַלְּצֵם׃

7

| | encampeth | The angel of | the LORD | round about | them that fear him, | and delivereth them. |

טַעֲמוּ וּרְאוּ כִּי־טוֹב יְהוָה אַשְׁרֵי הַגֶּבֶר יֶחֱסֶה־בּוֹ׃

8

| | O taste | and see | that | good: | the LORD *is* | blessed *is* | the man | *that* trusteth in him. |

יְראוּ אֶת־יְהוָה קְדֹשָׁיו כִּי־אֵין מַחְסוֹר לִירֵאָיו׃

9

| | O fear | the LORD, | ye his saints: | for *there is no* | want | to them that fear him. |

50

10 כְּפִירִים רָשׁוּ וְרָעֵבוּ וְדֹרְשֵׁי יְהוָה לֹא־יַחְסְרוּ כָל־טוֹב׃

The young lions do lack, and suffer hunger: but they that seek the LORD shall not want any good *thing*.

11 לְכוּ־בָנִים שִׁמְעוּ־לִי יִרְאַת יְהוָה אֲלַמֶּדְכֶם׃

Come, ye children, hearken unto me: the fear of the LORD I will teach you.

12 מִי־הָאִישׁ הֶחָפֵץ חַיִּים אֹהֵב יָמִים לִרְאוֹת טוֹב׃

What man *is he that* desireth life, *and* loveth *many* days, that he may see good?

13 נְצֹר לְשׁוֹנְךָ מֵרָע וּשְׂפָתֶיךָ מִדַּבֵּר מִרְמָה׃

Keep thy tongue from evil, and thy lips from speaking guile.

14 סוּר מֵרָע וַעֲשֵׂה־טוֹב בַּקֵּשׁ שָׁלוֹם וְרָדְפֵהוּ׃

Depart from evil, and do good; seek peace, and pursue it.

15 עֵינֵי יְהוָה אֶל־צַדִּיקִים וְאָזְנָיו אֶל־שַׁוְעָתָם׃

The eyes of the LORD *are* upon the righteous, and his ears *are open* unto their cry.

16 פְּנֵי יְהוָה בְּעֹשֵׂי רָע לְהַכְרִית מֵאֶרֶץ זִכְרָם׃

The face of the LORD *is against* them that do evil, to cut off the remembrance of them from the earth.

17 צָעֲקוּ וַיהוָה שָׁמֵעַ וּמִכָּל־צָרוֹתָם הִצִּילָם׃

The righteous cry, and the LORD heareth, and delivereth them out of all their troubles.

18 קָרוֹב יְהוָה לְנִשְׁבְּרֵי־לֵב וְאֶת־דַּכְּאֵי־רוּחַ יוֹשִׁיעַ׃

The LORD *is* nigh unto them that are of a broken heart; and saveth such as be of a contrite spirit.

19 רַבּוֹת רָעוֹת צַדִּיק וּמִכֻּלָּם יַצִּילֶנּוּ יְהוָה׃

Many *are the* afflictions of the righteous: but out of them all delivereth him the LORD.

20 שֹׁמֵר כָּל־עַצְמוֹתָיו אַחַת מֵהֵנָּה לֹא נִשְׁבָּרָה׃

He keepeth all his bones: one of them not is broken.

21 תְּמוֹתֵת רָשָׁע רָעָה וְשֹׂנְאֵי צַדִּיק יֶאְשָׁמוּ׃

Evil shall slay the wicked: and they that hate the righteous shall be desolate.

22 פּוֹדֶה יְהוָה נֶפֶשׁ עֲבָדָיו וְלֹא יֶאְשְׁמוּ כָּל־הַחֹסִים בּוֹ׃

The LORD redeemeth the soul of his servants: and none of them that trust [all] in him shall be desolate.

CAN YOU FIND THE "A-B-Cs"? - NO. 2

This Psalm is a little different. The first word is "Hallelujah," or "Praise the LORD." The first *alef* begins the next word. See if you can find the special way the alef-bet is used in this Psalm! By now you are remembering to read Hebrew from right to left.

Directions: Circle in pencil the first letter of each verse or phrase, noting the alphabetical order. Are all the letters of the alef-bet found? Are any missing?

Psalm 111

1 הַלְלוּ יָהּ אוֹדֶה יְהוָה בְּכָל־לֵבָב בְּסוֹד יְשָׁרִים וְעֵדָה׃

and *in* the congregation. / the upright, / in the assembly of / with *my* whole heart, / the LORD / I will praise / the LORD. / Praise ye

2 גְּדֹלִים מַעֲשֵׂי יְהוָה דְּרוּשִׁים לְכָל־חֶפְצֵיהֶם׃

of all them that have pleasure therein. / sought out / the LORD / The works of / *are* great,

3 הוֹד־וְהָדָר פָּעֳלוֹ וְצִדְקָתוֹ עֹמֶדֶת לָעַד׃

for ever. / endureth / and his righteousness / His work *is* / honourable and glorious:

4 זֵכֶר עָשָׂה לְנִפְלְאֹתָיו חַנּוּן וְרַחוּם יְהוָה׃

the LORD *is* / and full of compassion. / gracious / his wonderful works / He hath made / to be remembered:

5 טֶרֶף נָתַן לִירֵאָיו יִזְכֹּר לְעוֹלָם בְּרִיתוֹ׃

of his covenant. / ever / he will be mindful / unto them that fear him: / He hath given / meat

6 כֹּחַ מַעֲשָׂיו הִגִּיד לְעַמּוֹ לָתֵת לָהֶם נַחֲלַת גּוֹיִם׃

of the heathen. / the heritage / them / that he may give / his people, / he hath shewed / his works / The power of

7 מַעֲשֵׂי יָדָיו אֱמֶת וּמִשְׁפָּט נֶאֱמָנִים כָּל־פִּקּוּדָיו׃

all his commandments / *are* sure. / and judgment; / *are* verity / his hands / The works of

8 סְמוּכִים לָעַד לְעוֹלָם עֲשׂוּיִם בֶּאֱמֶת וְיָשָׁר׃

and uprightness. / in truth / *and are* done / and ever, / for ever / They stand fast

9 פְּדוּת שָׁלַח לְעַמּוֹ צִוָּה־לְעוֹלָם בְּרִיתוֹ קָדוֹשׁ וְנוֹרָא שְׁמוֹ׃

is his name. / and reverend / holy / his covenant / for ever: / he hath commanded / unto his people: / He sent / redemption

10 רֵאשִׁית חָכְמָה יִרְאַת יְהוָה שֵׂכֶל טוֹב לְכָל־עֹשֵׂיהֶם תְּהִלָּתוֹ עֹמֶדֶת לָעַד׃

for ever. / endureth / his praise / that do *his* commandments: / have all they / a good understanding / the LORD / The fear of / wisdom: / *is* the beginning of

52

CAN YOU FIND THE "A-B-Cs"? – NO. 3

Circle the "alef-bet" (first letter of each verse) in order from verse one through verse twenty-one. The arrow shows you where to begin. Are any of the letters missing? Which one(s)?

Psalm 145

1 : וָעֶד לְעוֹלָם שִׁמְךָ וַאֲבָרְכָה הַמֶּלֶךְ אֱלוֹהַי אֲרוֹמִמְךָ לְדָוִד תְּהִלָּה

and ever. | for ever | thy name | and I will bless | O king; | my God, | I will extol thee, | David's | *Psalm* of praise.

2 : וָעֶד לְעוֹלָם שִׁמְךָ וַאֲהַלְלָה אֲבָרְכֶךָּ בְּכָל־יוֹם

and ever. | for ever | thy name | and I will praise | will I bless thee; | Every day

3 : חֵקֶר אֵין וְלִגְדֻלָּתוֹ מְאֹד וּמְהֻלָּל יְהוָה גָּדוֹל

searchable. | *is* not | and his greatness | greatly; | and to be praised | the LORD, | Great *is*

4 : יַגִּידוּ וּגְבוּרֹתֶיךָ מַעֲשֶׂיךָ יְשַׁבַּח לְדוֹר דּוֹר

shall declare. | and thy mighty acts | thy works | shall praise | to another, | One generation

5 : אָשִׂיחָה נִפְלְאֹתֶיךָ וְדִבְרֵי הוֹדֶךָ כְּבוֹד הֲדַר

I will speak. | thy wondrous works | and the things of | of thy majesty, | of the glory | Of the honour

6 : אֲסַפְּרֶנָּה וּגְדוּלָּתֶיךָ יֹאמֵרוּ נוֹרְאֹתֶיךָ וֶעֱזוּז

I will declare. | and thy greatness | *men* shall speak of; | thy terrible acts | And the might of

7 : יְרַנֵּנוּ וְצִדְקָתְךָ יַבִּיעוּ רַב־טוּבְךָ זֵכֶר

shall sing. | and of thy righteousness | They shall abundantly utter | thy great goodness, | the memory of

8 : חָסֶד וּגְדָל־ אַפַּיִם אֶרֶךְ יְהוָה וְרַחוּם חַנּוּן

and of great mercy. | anger, | slow to | The LORD *is* | and full of compassion; | gracious,

9 : מַעֲשָׂיו עַל־כָּל־ וְרַחֲמָיו לַכֹּל יְהוָה טוֹב־

his works. | *are* over all | and his tender mercies | to all: | The LORD *is* | good

10 : יְבָרְכוּכָה וַחֲסִידֶיךָ כָּל־מַעֲשֶׂיךָ יְהוָה יוֹדוּךָ

shall bless thee. | and thy saints | All thy works | O LORD; | shall praise thee,

11 : יְדַבֵּרוּ וּגְבוּרָתְךָ יֹאמֵרוּ מַלְכוּתְךָ כְּבוֹד

talk of; | and thy power | They shall speak of | thy kingdom, | the glory of

53

12 לְהוֹדִיעַ לִבְנֵי הָאָדָם גְּבוּרֹתָיו וּכְבוֹד הֲדַר מַלְכוּתוֹ :

To make known | to the sons of | men | his mighty acts, | and the glorious | majesty of | his kingdom.

13 מַלְכוּתְךָ מַלְכוּת כָּל־עֹלָמִים וּמֶמְשַׁלְתְּךָ בְּכָל־דּוֹר וָדוֹר :

Thy kingdom | is a kingdom | everlasting, | and thy dominion | endureth throughout all generations.

14 סוֹמֵךְ יְהוָה לְכָל־הַנֹּפְלִים וְזוֹקֵף לְכָל־הַכְּפוּפִים :

upholdeth | The LORD | all that fall, | and raiseth up | all those that be bowed down.

15 עֵינֵי־כֹל אֵלֶיךָ יְשַׂבֵּרוּ וְאַתָּה נוֹתֵן־לָהֶם אֶת־אָכְלָם בְּעִתּוֹ :

The eyes of | all | upon thee; | wait | and thou | givest them | their meat | in due season.

16 פּוֹתֵחַ אֶת־יָדֶךָ וּמַשְׂבִּיעַ לְכָל־חַי רָצוֹן :

Thou openest | thine hand, | and satisfiest | of every living thing. | the desire

17 צַדִּיק יְהוָה בְּכָל־דְּרָכָיו וְחָסִיד בְּכָל־מַעֲשָׂיו :

righteous | The LORD is | in all his ways, | and holy [lit. kind] | in all his works.

18 קָרוֹב יְהוָה לְכָל־קֹרְאָיו לְכֹל אֲשֶׁר יִקְרָאֻהוּ בֶאֱמֶת :

is nigh | The LORD | unto all them that call upon him, | to all | that | call upon him | in truth.

19 רְצוֹן־יְרֵאָיו יַעֲשֶׂה וְאֶת־שַׁוְעָתָם יִשְׁמַע וְיוֹשִׁיעֵם :

the desire of | them that fear him: | He will fulfil | and their cry | will hear, | he also | and will save them.

20 שׁוֹמֵר יְהוָה אֶת־כָּל־אֹהֲבָיו וְאֵת כָּל־הָרְשָׁעִים יַשְׁמִיד :

preserveth | The LORD | all them that love him: | but | all the wicked | will he destroy.

21 תְּהִלַּת יְהוָה יְדַבֶּר־פִּי וִיבָרֵךְ כָּל־בָּשָׂר שֵׁם קָדְשׁוֹ לְעוֹלָם וָעֶד :

the praise of | the LORD: | My mouth | shall speak | and bless | let all flesh | his holy | name | for ever | and ever.

In some versions of the Old Testament, יהוה is translated as "Jehovah." The word יהוה is not pronounced by the Jews, so each time יהוה occurs in the manuscripts, it is usually read as "Adonai."

If you don't own a copy of a Hebrew-English Interlinear Old Testament, make sure you order one; this is a MUST if you would study the Hebrew Scriptures! Copies of the Hebrew-English Interlinear Old Testament can be purchased online either in one large volume, or smaller volume sets.

If you are interested in examining more "alphabetical" chapters in the Tanach, see Psalm 25; Psalm 119 (same beginning letter for every eight verses); Psalm 112 (consecutive alef-bet letters for every half verse); Proverbs 31:10-31; and Lamentations 1; 2; 4; and Lamentations 3 (same letter for every three verses).

NOTES ON THE HEBREW ALEF-BET/ALPHABET

(Squared Script)

alef

✿ This first letter is a vowel, but makes no sound when alone, or at the end of a word.

✿ Alef only makes a sound when seen with one of these "vowel points":

(֡ – ֺֺ ֹ ֗ ֺ֗ ֺ)

(The names of these vowels are shown on page 49.)

For example, אָ sounds like "ah" as in *father*. When you see a ֡ under an alef in modern Hebrew, it also sounds like "ah." The word for *nose* is אָף "ahf."

✿ The letter has a numerical value of 1.

bet/vet

✿ This second letter (ב), with a dot inside, sounds like the English "b." בָּ is "bah," as in *bother*. The vet, (ב) "v"- sound, does not have a dot inside.

✿ בְ can be prefixed to a word, and means *in, into, inside*, or *on*, and *with*. For example: "And the king held out to Esther the golden scepter which was **in his hand**." (בְּיָדוֹ) Esther 5:2 NKJV™. (Only the *italicized* words here are translated into Hebrew.) Circle the letter in the above Hebrew phrase that means "in."

✿ This letter's numerical value is 2.

gimel

✿ The gimel sounds like a hard "g" as in *go*. There are NO soft g sounds in Hebrew! —NO "g" as in *giants*!

✿ Do not worry about the various pronunciations for the names of the letters themselves, as Jews around the world will say them differently. (The Sephardic Jews might pronounce this "geemel" and others might say "gimmel," etc.) But it IS important to know the sound the letter makes!

✿ The numerical value is 3.

dalet

✿ Dalet sounds like "d"as in *dog*.

✿ דֶּלֶת "DEH-let" means *door*, and if you notice how a ד is written, it appears as a doorpost on the right side and a lintel across the top of a door.

✿ With either a ֡ or a ֵ under the ד, the pronunciation is the same: דָ is "dah"; דֶ is "dah."

✿ The numerical value is 4.

hay

- ✿ This letter is the "h" sound, as in *hot*. The word for *behold* is "hay" (הֵא) or "heenay" (הִנֵּה).
- ✿ See the *Heenay Ma Tohv* song on the ט (tet) picture page.
- ✿ When הַ is prefixed to a word, it means *the*. *The father* is הָאַבָּא; *the door* is הַדֶּלֶת. See the ה picture page, p.11, for more "hay" words.
- ✿ The numerical value of ה is 5.

vahv

- ✿ This letter is pronounced like a "v."
- ✿ This letter is most often used as a prefix to a word to mean *and*. Example: "*Father and mother*" (אַבָּא וְאִמָּא). See the vahv picture page. Since the word vahv (וָו) literally means *hook* or *nail*, it is easy to see how you have the idea of hooking two words together with the conjunction "and."
- ✿ Remember to read from right to left in Hebrew!
- ✿ This letter vahv (ו) is interesting in other ways: Vahv with a dot (kholam) above (וֹ) says "oh," and is now a vowel. The word *Torah*, the word for the first five books of the Bible, has this kind of vahv: *the toh-RAH* (הַתּוֹרָה). *Day* (יוֹם) "yohm" also has a vahv with kholam (a dot).
- ✿ When וֹ is added on the end of a word, it means "his." Example: "Oh, give thanks to the God of heaven, for **His mercy** (חַסְדּוֹ) "khahs-DOH" endures forever." Psalm 136:26 NKJV™.
- ✿ When a vahv has a dot in the middle of it (וּ), we say "oo" as in *spoon*. הוּא is pronounced "hoo," but means *he*.
- ✿ This letter has a numerical value of six.

zayin

- ✿ Zayin sounds like "z" as in *zebra*.
- ✿ A segol (ֶ) under a letter adds an "eh" sound. Example: זֶה "Zeh" means *this*.
- ✿ The verb זָמַר "zah-MAHR" means, "*to prune, to pluck with the fingers on a musical instrument,*" or "*sing praises.*" (See verse on page 14).
- ✿ This letter has a numerical value of seven.

✿ This letter is an "h" but with a guttural sound from the back of the throat, like the "ch" in the name of the composer J. S. Bach. So, every time you see the "ch" or "kh" in the pronunciations by the Hebrew word in this book, please give it the guttural "ch" as in Bach's name, and NEVER a "ch" as in "church"!

✿ The similarity in looks of a "hay" (ה) and a "khet" (ח) must be observed and practiced in writing, the "hay" being open and the "khet" closed.

✿ The word for *brother* is אָח, said much like an exclamation made when something goes wrong - "Ach!"

✿ This letter has a numerical value of eight.

khet

✿ Tet sounds as a "t."

✿ טוב "tohv," the word for *good*, starts with tet. Remember—read from right to left!

✿ This letter has a numerical value of nine.

tet

✿ Yud is a small apostrophe-like letter which has the "y" sound, as in *yes*.

✿ Combined with the vowels, we say: יָ = "yah"; יָד = "yahd"; יִ = "yee"; יַ = "yay"; יַ = "yah"; יְ = y' (a short yeh); יֶ = "yeh"

✿ The exception to this is when yud follows a letter with a dot under it. For example: הִי = "hee"; בִּי ="bee"; דִי ="dee"; כִּי = "key"; מִי = "mee"

✿ When the yud is added to the end of a word, it can mean *my*. For example: ..."**And My people** (וְעַמִּי) shall be satisfied with **My goodness** (טוּבִי) says the LORD." Jeremiah 31:14 NKJV™. Circle the letter that can mean "my."

✿ This letter has a numerical value of ten.

yud

✿ כ (kaf) *with* a dot, or dagesh, has the sound of our letter k.

✿ כ (khaf) *without* a dot, has the sound of the "ch" in J. S. Bach's name. Practice saying the guttural khaf (כ) over and over!

✿ ך at the end of a word is a *final khaf*, or *khaf sofit* (so-FEET), said with the same throaty sound as a regular *khaf*.

✿ When a ך is added to the end of a word, it indicates the pronoun *your* or *thy*. For example: "Oh, LORD, I have remembered **Your name** (שְׁמֶךָ) in the night and have kept **Your law**." (תּוֹרָתֶךָ) Psalm 119:55.

✿ Circle the letter which can mean *your* or *thy*.

✿ כ when prefixed to a word, means *like, as, according to*. Example: "Lo, nations are **as a drop** (כְּמַר) from a bucket, and are reckoned **as dust** (כְּשַׁחַק) of the scales." Isaiah 40:15. Circle the letter that can mean *like* or *as*.

✿ The word for *yes* (כֵּן) begins with this letter.

✿ This letter has a numerical value of 20.

kaf/khaf/final khaf

lamed

✿ The lamed sounds like "l" as in *love*.

✿ The words *God* (אֵל) and *to* (אֶל) are both said today as "el."

✿ The word for *no*, or *not*, is pronounced "lo" (לֹא). "You shall **not** (לֹא) have any other gods besides Me." Exodus 20:3.

✿ The word for *why?* is "lah-MAH" (לָמָה?).

✿ When ל is prefixed to a word, it means *to, toward, belonging to, for*. Examples: "And the child grew, and she brought him **to the daughter** (לְבַת) of Pharoah, and he became a son **to her** (לָהּ), and she called his name Moses..." Exodus 2:10. "And it shall come to pass in that day, the LORD shall hiss **for the fly** (לַזְבוּב) that is in the end of the rivers of Egypt, **and for the bee** (וְלַדְּבוֹרָה) that is in the land of Assyria." Isaiah 7:18. Circle the letter in each Hebrew word which can mean *to* or *for*.

✿ The numerical value of this letter is 30.

mem/final mem

✿ This letter has an "m" sound as in *mama*.

✿ מַה? "Mah" means *what?* מִי? "Mee" is the word *who?*

✿ מִן "Min" is the word *from, out of*. Example: "And a mist went up **from the earth** (מִן־הָאָרֶץ) and watered the whole face of the ground." Genesis 2:6.

✿ מִ is short for the word *from* and is often prefixed to a Hebrew word. Example: "And He rested on the seventh day **from all** (מִכָּל) His work which He had made." Genesis 2:2. Circle the letter which means *from*.

✿ Example of final mems in Jeremiah 25:14: "**many nations** (גּוֹיִם רַבִּים) and **great kings**" (וּמְלָכִים גְדוֹלִים). Notice that the adjectives *many* and *great* have plural endings that agree with their masculine plural nouns, *nations* and *kings*.

✿ The numerical value of this letter is 40.

nun/final nun

✿ Nun (pronounced "noon") has the "n" sound, as in *Noah*.

✿ The word for *please* or *I pray thee* is נָא "nah." "And he called to her and said, **Please** (נָא) bring to me a little water in a vessel and I shall drink." 1 Kings 17:10.

✿ The word for *son* (בֵּן) "ben," has the final form of nun.

✿ This letter has a numerical value of 50.

samek

- ✿ This letter has the "s" sound as in *Samuel.*
- ✿ ס (Samek) sounds similar to the verb "samach" (סָמַךְ), which means *support, uphold.* It is used in Psalm 145:14 NKJV™: "The LORD **upholds** (סוֹמֵךְ) all those who fall, and raises up all who are bowed down."
- ✿ The numerical value of this letter is 60.

ayin

- ✿ This letter, like the א, carries no sound (is silent) unless accompanied by a vowel.
- ✿ The letter ע is pronounced "AH-yeen" (עַיִן), and actually means *eye.* "Rivers of water run down **my eyes** (עֵינָי) for they keep not Your law." Psalm 119:136.
- ✿ The great "Shemah" of the Law in Deuteronomy 6:4, 5 (NKJV™) ends with this letter ע. "**Hear**, (שְׁמַע) O Israel: the LORD our God, the LORD is one! You shall love the LORD your God with all your heart, with all your soul, and with all your might." Strong's *Exhaustive Concordance of the Bible* indicates the "shemah" means to "listen with the intent of obedience and diligence." (#8085).
- ✿ The numerical value of this letter is 70.

pay/fay/final fay

- ✿ This letter פ with a dot (dagesh) sounds as the p in *palm.* The "fay" פ (without a dot) sounds as an "f."
- ✿ פֶה is pronounced "peh," and has the meaning of *mouth.*
- ✿ When appearing at the end of a word, the "fay" looks like ף and is said as an "f." Joseph's name would be an example: יוֹסֵף "YOH-sehf."
- ✿ The word *wonderful, miracle* begins with the "pay": "For to us a Child is born, to us a Son is given; and the princely power shall be on His shoulder; and His name shall be called **Wonderful** (פֶלֶא) ["PEH-leh"]..." Isaiah 9:6
- ✿ The numerical value of this letter is 80.

tsadee/tsadee sofit

- ✿ This letter has the "ts" sound as in the word *hats.*
- ✿ When a tsadee comes at the end of a word, it looks like ץ.
- ✿ The word for *tree* (עֵץ) "ayts," ends with a final tsadee (tsadee sofit).
- ✿ "Tsadee" is close in sound to "tsadeek," which means *righteous, (or righteous person).* "For the LORD knows the way of the **righteous** (צַדִּיקִים - plural form), but the way of the ungodly shall perish." Psalm 1:6 NKJV™.
- ✿ The numerical value of this letter is 90.

kuf

✿ Kuf sounds like "k" as in *kite*.

✿ The verb, *to call, cry, proclaim* begins with this letter, as in Jeremiah 33:3: *"**Call** (קְרָא) to Me, and I will answer you and tell you great and inscrutible things, you do not know them."*

✿ The numerical value to this letter is 100.

reysh

✿ Reysh has the "r" sound, as in *return*. However, each time you see a reysh in Hebrew, "roll" the r's slightly.

✿ *Head* begins with this letter, as in Deuteronomy 28:13 NKJV™: "And the LORD will make you the **head** (רֹאשׁ) ["rohsh"] and not the tail..."

✿ "Rohsh" can also mean *highest* or *chief*, as in Exodus 12:2: "This month shall be the **chief** (רֹאשׁ) of months for you; it shall be the **first** (רִאשׁוֹן) of the months of the year for you."

✿ The word *great* starts with the letter reysh, as in Lamentations 3:23: "**Great** (רַבָּה) ["ra-BAH"] is Your faithfulness."

✿ The numerical value is 200.

seen/sheen

✿ The letter "seen" (with a dot on the left side), has the sound of "s" as in *say*.

✿ *Prince, ruler, master* is "sar," as in Hosea 3:4: "For the sons of Israel shall stay many days with no king, and no **prince** (שַׂר), and with no sacrifice and no pillars, and no ephod or teraphim."

✿ "Sheen" (with a dot over the right side) has the "sh" sound, as in *ship*. The word for *tooth* is "shane" (שֵׁן).

✿ The numerical value is 300.

tahv

✿ In these modern times, the tahv is sounded as a "t," like in *top*.

✿ Originally, the letter was written more as the shape of a cross or "x" and meant *mark* or *sign*.

✿ "Tahv" (תָו) is used twice in the Old Testament with this meaning, once in Ezekiel 9:4: "Pass through in the midst of the city, in the midst of Jerusalem, and mark a **mark** (תָו) on the foreheads of the men who are groaning and are mourning over all the abominations that are done in her midst."

✿ The numerical value of tahv is 400.

AN "ALEF-BET" OF VERBS

Almost all verbs are composed of 3-letter roots. Learn the verb roots. The way a verb is used in a sentence will determine its spelling, but the 3-letter root will always be evident. Below are samples of basic verbs to begin adding to your vocabulary. There is one for every letter of the alef-bet. Begin this section only in WEEK 19 (See Lesson Plans). Circle each of the 3 letters in the root word. (The first one is done for you.) Remember to start reading the Hebrew sentences from the right and proceed to the left!

"And I will delight myself in Your commandments, which I have loved." Psalm 119:47

⇦ וְאֶשְׁתַּעֲשַׁע בְּמִצְוֹתֶיךָ אֲשֶׁר אָהָבְתִּי

Do you see the 3-letter Hebrew root for "love" in the example above?
The ending תִּי (tee) indicates the first person (I), and an action in the past tense. Find and circle the 3-letter roots in each example from here on. Hint: the letters may be "hidden" by prefixes, infixes, or suffixes. An example of each will be given in this section.

א.ה.ב
(ah-HAHV)
root for
"love"

I love you! (ahn-EE oh-HEH-vet oht-KHAH)   אֲנִי אוֹהֶבֶת אֹתְךָ

(Circle the root letters for "love.") This is a female speaking to a male.
Example of an infix: In "love" above, the vowel (וֹ) is inserted after the alef (א), and tells us that the verb is in the present tense.

✿   ✿   ✿

We (are) building a small house.   אֲנַחְנוּ בּוֹנִים בַּיִת קָטָן

Example of a suffix: In the verb "are building" above, the יִם (eem) is added at the end of the verb, בּוֹנֶה, to tell us the verb is masculine in gender, and plural (we). (Circle the root letters.) (The letter *hay* has been replaced by the plural ending, *eem*.)

Noah built the ark. (Circle the verb root.)   נֹחַ בָּנָה אֶת הַתֵּבָה

ב.נ.ה
(bah-NAH)
root for
"build"

"And they said, 'Come, let us build for ourselves a city and a tower...'" Genesis 11:4a
(Circle the verb root letters for "build.")

וַיֹּאמְרוּ הָבָה נִבְנֶה-לָּנוּ עִיר וּמִגְדָּל....

ג

ג.נ.ב
(gah-NAHV)
root for
"steal"

ד

ד.ב.ר
(dah-BAHR)
root for
"speak," "say"

ה

ה.ל.ך
(hah-LACH)
root for
"go," "walk"

ן

(Remember to circle the verb roots in each example.)

"Thou shalt not steal." Exodus 20:15 KJV ⇦ לֹא תִגְנֹב

The boy stole (an) apple. הַיֶּלֶד גָּנַב תַּפּוּחַ

✡   ✡   ✡

"He spoke to them in the cloudy pillar." Psalm 99:7 בְּעַמּוּד עָנָן יְדַבֵּר אֲלֵיהֶם

She is speaking softly. הִיא מְדַבֶּרֶת בְּרַכּוּת

✡   ✡   ✡

I went to the city. הָלַכְתִּי לָעִיר

Note: The khaf in this example is not at the end of the word, so we use a 'regular' khaf, and NOT a final khaf. (See arrow.)

"Blessed is the man *who has not walked* in the counsel of the wicked." Psalm 1:1
Note: Only the words in *italics* are translated into Hebrew.

.... אֲשֶׁר לֹא הָלַךְ ....

✡   ✡   ✡

Although the vahvs below are not actually a part of the verbs, they are known as "vahv conversives." The examples begin with a vahv ("and"), followed by a yud, and always indicate that a verb is coming. These "vahv conversives" assume pronouns in the third person, such as "he," "it," or "they." The verbs here are in the past tense.

"...and he sent..." Numbers 22:5 וַיִּשְׁלַח

"...and he died." Genesis 5:5 וַיָּמָת

"...and He saved them." Psalm 106:10 וַיּוֹשִׁיעֵם

"...and the LORD called Moses." Exodus 19:20b KJV וַיִּקְרָא יְהֹוָה לְמֹשֶׁה

"And God spoke to Noah..." Genesis 8:15 וַיְדַבֵּר אֱלֹהִים אֶל־נֹחַ

"...and [they] arose..." Genesis 37:35 וַיָּקֻמוּ

62

ז

ז.כ.ר

(zah-KHAR)
root for
"remember"

ח

ח.י.ם

(khah-YAHM)
root for "live"

ט

ט.ע.ם

(tah-AHM)
root for
"taste"

י

י.ד.ע

(yah-DAH)
root for
"know"

כ

כ.ת.ב

(kah-TAHV)
root for
"write"

"Remember now your Creator, in the days of your youth." Ecclesiastes 12:1

⇦ וּזְכֹר אֶת־בּוֹרְאֶךָ בִּימֵי בְּחוּרֹתֶיךָ

Example of a prefix, above: The vowel vahv (וּ), (pronounced "oo"), in front of זְכֹר, means "and." (Remember to circle all verb roots on this page.)

"I remembered the LORD." Jonah 2:7 NKJV™   אֶת־יְהֹוָה זָכַרְתִּי

✡ ✡ ✡

..."but I shall live." Psalm 118:17   כִּי־אֶחְיֶה

He lives in my heart.   הוּא חַי בְּלִבִּי

✡ ✡ ✡

"Oh, taste and see that the LORD is good." Psalm 34:8 NKJV™

טַעֲמוּ וּרְאוּ כִּי־טוֹב יְהֹוָה

I tasted the fruits.   אֲנִי טָעַמְתִּי אֶת הַפֵּרוֹת

✡ ✡ ✡

"And Jacob awakened from his sleep and said, 'Surely the LORD is in this place, *and I did not know it.'*" Genesis 28:16 NKJV™   ....וְאָנֹכִי לֹא יָדָעְתִּי....

We know that you speak the truth.   אֲנַחְנוּ יוֹדְעִים אַתָּה מְדַבֵּר אֱמֶת

✡ ✡ ✡

"And the LORD said to Moses, *'Write this, (for) a memorial in the book...'*"
Exodus 17:14 NKJV™   ....כְּתֹב זֹאת זִכְרוֹן בַּסֵּפֶר....

She is writing to her mother.   הִיא כּוֹתֶבֶת לְאִמָּא

ל
ל.מ.ד
(lah-MAHD)
root for
"learn"

"Learn to do good." Isaiah 1:17 ⇐ לִמְדוּ הֵיטֵב (Circle all verb roots on this page.)

I am learning from the book. אֲנִי לוֹמֵד מִן הַסֵּפֶר

✿ ✿ ✿

"But of the tree of the knowledge of good and evil, you may not eat, *for in the day that you eat of it, you shall surely die.*" Genesis 2:17 NKJV™
Can you find and circle the double verb (used for emphasis) in the example below?

....כִּי בְּיוֹם אֲכָלְךָ מִמֶּנּוּ מוֹת תָּמוּת

מ
מ.ו.ת
(mah-VET)
root for
"die"

"For the youth shall die the son of a hundred years..." Isaiah 65:20

כִּי הַנַּעַר בֶּן־מֵאָה שָׁנָה יָמוּת

✿ ✿ ✿

"And she gave to the king a hundred and twenty talents of gold, and very many spices, and precious stones; no spice like that came any more for abundance, *that the Queen of Sheba gave to King Solomon.*" I Kings 10:10 (Note: In this example, the verb has a feminine ending.) ....אֲשֶׁר־נָתְנָה מַלְכַּת־שְׁבָא לַמֶּלֶךְ שְׁלֹמֹה

נ
נ.ת.ן
(nah-TAHN)
root for
"give"

He is giving a book to the man. הוּא נוֹתֵן אֶת הַסֵּפֶר לָאִישׁ

✿ ✿ ✿

"And the LORD shut him in." Genesis 7:16 NKJV™ literally - "And shut the LORD behind him." וַיִּסְגֹּר יְהוָה בַּעֲדוֹ

ס
ס.ג.ר
(sah-GAHR)
root for
"shut"

"My God has sent His Angel, *and He has shut the lion's mouths,* and they have not hurt me." Daniel 6:22 ....וּסֲגַר פֻּם אַרְיָוָתָא

✿ ✿ ✿

"So I prophesied as He commanded me, and the breath came into them. *And they lived, and stood on their feet, a very, very great army.*" Ezekiel 37:10

....וַיִּחְיוּ וַיַּעַמְדוּ עַל־רַגְלֵיהֶם חַיִל גָּדוֹל מְאֹד מְאֹד

ע
ע.מ.ד
(ah-MAHD)
root for
"stand"

"He casts out His ice like crumbs; *who can stand before His cold?*" Psalm 147:17
literally - "...Before His cold who can stand?" לִפְנֵי קָרָתוֹ מִי יַעֲמֹד

64

פ

פ.ד.ה

(pah-DAH)

root for
"redeem,"
"save,"
"deliver"

צ

צ.פ.ה

(tsa-FAH)

root for
"watch,"
"observe"

ק

ק.ר.א

(kah-RAH)

root for
"call,"
"cry,"
"read,"
"proclaim"

"Redeem Israel, O God, out of all his troubles." Psalm 25:22

⇐ פְּדֵה־אֱלֹהִים אֶת־יִשְׂרָאֵל מִכֹּל צָרוֹתָיו

"...and every firstborn of men among your sons you shall redeem." Exodus 13:13b

.... וְכֹל בְּכֹר אָדָם בְּבָנֶיךָ תִּפְדֶּה

✿ ✿ ✿

"May the LORD watch between you and me, when we are absent one from another."
Genesis 31:49 NKJV™ Notice the final fay (ף).

יִצֶף יְהוָה בֵּינִי וּבֵינֶךָ כִּי נִסָּתֵר אִישׁ מֵרֵעֵהוּ

"And you, son of man, I have set you as a watchman to the house of Israel..." Ezekiel 33:7

Note: Here "watchman," a noun, comes from the verb "watch."

.... וְאַתָּה בֶן־אָדָם צֹפֶה נְתַתִּיךָ לְבֵית יִשְׂרָאֵל

✿ ✿ ✿

"And call upon Me in the day of trouble; I will deliver you, and you shall glorify Me."
Psalm 50:15 NKJV™

.... וּקְרָאֵנִי בְּיוֹם צָרָה

"Cry aloud, for he is a god; either he is meditating, or he is busy, or he is on a journey, or perhaps he is sleeping and must be awakened." I Kings 18:27 NKJV™

.... קִרְאוּ בְקוֹל־גָּדוֹל כִּי־אֱלֹהִים

"And they stood up in their place and read in the Book of the Law of the LORD."
Nehemiah 9:3

.... וַיָּקוּמוּ עַל־עָמְדָם וַיִּקְרְאוּ בְּסֵפֶר תּוֹרַת יְהוָה

"The Spirit of the LORD God is upon Me, because the Lord has anointed Me to preach good tidings to the poor; He has sent Me to heal the brokenhearted, *to proclaim liberty to the captives..."* Isaiah 61:1 NKJV™

.... לִקְרֹא לִשְׁבוּיִם דְּרוֹר

ר

ר.א.ה

(rah-AH)

root for
"look,"
"see,"
"behold"

"And she [Hannah] vowed a vow, and said, 'O LORD of hosts, *if You will certainly look upon the affliction of Your servant,* and shall remember me, and shall not forget Your servant, and shall give to Your servant a man child, then I will give him to the LORD all the days of his life, and a razor shall not go upon his head.'" I Samuel 1:11

Hint: There is a double verb here, for emphasis. Circle both verb roots.

⇦ .... אִם־רָאֹה תִרְאֶה בָּעֳנִי אֲמָתֶךָ ....

"Watch the perfect and behold the upright; for the end of (that) man (is) peace." Psalm 37:37

שְׁמָר־תָּם וּרְאֵה יָשָׁר כִּי־אַחֲרִית לְאִישׁ שָׁלוֹם:

"He has no form or comeliness; *and when we see Him,* there is no beauty that we should desire Him." Isaiah 53:2b NKJV™   וְנִרְאֵהוּ ....

✡   ✡   ✡

שׁ

שׁ.מ.ר

(shah-MAHR)

root for
"guard,"
"keep"

"For He shall give His angels charge over you, to keep you in all your ways." Psalm 91:11

כִּי מַלְאָכָיו יְצַוֶּה־לָּךְ לִשְׁמָרְךָ בְּכָל־דְּרָכֶיךָ:

"Unless the LORD builds the house, they labor in vain who build it; *Unless the LORD guards the city,* the watchman stays awake in vain." Psalm 127:1 NKJV™

.... אִם־יְהוָה לֹא־יִשְׁמָר־עִיר ....

"My son, keep My words and store up My commandments within you." Proverbs 7:1

בְּנִי שְׁמֹר אֲמָרָי וּמִצְוֹתַי תִּצְפֹּן אִתָּךְ:

✡   ✡   ✡

ת

ת.פ.ר

(tah-FAHR)

root for
"sew,"
"stitch"

"And the eyes of them both were opened, and they knew that they were naked, *and they sewed leaves of the fig tree and made girdles for themselves.*" Genesis 3:7

.... וַיִּתְפְּרוּ עֲלֵה תְאֵנָה וַיַּעֲשׂוּ לָהֶם חֲגֹרֹת

"...a time to tear, and a time to sew together." Ecclesiastes 3:7

.... עֵת לִקְרוֹעַ וְעֵת לִתְפּוֹר:

WRITING PRACTICE FOR THE HEBREW "ALEF-BET"

Divide this section of the book into two parts. Practice drawing each (single) letter of the "alef-bet" in the first weeks of your study. The arrow tells you where to begin. After you have mastered writing each letter of the alef-bet at the **top half** of this page, then come back (during Weeks 11 and 12) and write the words at the bottom half of these pages. Take your time and do a great job! (Note: You may copy these writing practice pages, one for each student in your family, if needed.)

alef   א

After you have practiced writing the *bet* on the next page, come back and practice writing the Hebrew word for *father* or *daddy* (AH-bah):   אַבָּא

Stop! Do the rest of this page in Week 11.
From the picture section of the book, choose two more words which begin with *alef* and practice writing them here.

Practice Page for Bet and Vet

Practice writing the letters *bet* and *vet*.
The arrow tells you where to begin.

בּ

bet, "b" sound

After you have practiced writing the letters bet, gimel, and dalet,
practice writing the Hebrew word for *garment* or *dress*: "BEH-gehd."

בֶּגֶד

Stop! Wait until Week 13 to do this one.
Choose two more words that begin with *bet* and write them here.

vet, "v" sound

ב

Practice Page for Gimel

Practice writing the letter *gimel*. It has the "g" sound, as in "go."
The arrow tells you where to begin.

Stop! Wait to do the rest of the page until Week 13.
Practice writing the Hebrew word for *garden* here:

Choose two more words which start with *gimel* and practice below.

Practice Page for Dalet

Practice writing the letter *dalet*, which has a "d" sound.
The arrow tells you where to begin.

ד

Make right side of horizontal line overlap vertical line. ↘ ↓

Practice writing the Hebrew word for *fish*:

דָּג

Stop! Wait until Week 15 to do this exercise.
Choose two words that begin with *dalet* and practice writing them below.

Practice Page for Hay

Practice writing the *hay*, which has a "h" sound.
The arrow tells you where to begin.

ה

↓

Be sure lines DO NOT touch. → ⌐ ⌐

Stop! Wait until week 11 to do this word.
Practice writing the word for *mountain* below.

הַר

Stop! Wait until week 15 to do the rest of the page.
Choose two more words which start with *hay* and write them here.

Practice Page for Vahv

Practice writing the letter *vahv*, which has the "v" sound.
The arrow tells you where to begin.

Draw the horizontal line very short.

Stop! Wait for Week 17 to do this.
Vahv is the letter for "and." Find and write the Hebrew words *father and mother.*
(Always practice them at least five times).

Practice Page for Zayin

Practice writing the letter *zayin*, which has a "z" sound.
The arrow tells you where to begin.

זֵ

Practice writing the word for *gold* here.

זָהָב

Stop! Wait until Week 17 to do this one.
Choose two more words that begin with *zayin* and write them below.

Practice Page for Khet

Practice writing the *khet*, which sounds like a guttural "h." See p. 57.
The arrow tells you where to begin.

ח

Be sure lines touch! ↗

Stop! Wait to do the rest of this page until Week 19.
<u>Write the Hebrew word for *friend* below.</u>

חָבֵר

<u>Write two more words that start with *khet*.</u>

Practice Page for Tet

Practice writing *tet*, which has a "t" sound.
The arrows tell you where to begin.

ט

Stop! Wait until Week 19 to do the rest of the page.
Write the word for *baker* below.

טַבָּח

Write two more words that begin with the letter *tet*.

Practice Page for Yud

Practice writing *yud*, which has a "y" sound.
The arrow tells you where to begin.

ד

יד
ָ

_____

Practice writing the word for *hand*.

_____

Stop! Wait until Week 21 to do this.
Choose two more words that begin with *yud* and write them on this page.

_____

_____

_____

_____

_____

_____

_____

_____

Practice Page for Kaf, Khaf, and Khaf Sofit

Practice writing *kaf*, *khaf*, and *khaf sofit*.
The arrow tells you where to begin.

כּ

kaf, "k" sound

כָּבוֹד

Write the word for *glory*.

כ

khaf, guttural "ch" or "kh" sound

ך

khaf (final or sofit), guttural "ch" or "kh" sound

Stop! Wait until Week 21 to do this one.
Example of final khaf - "your commands" - Psalm 119:6.

מִצְוֺתֶךָ

Practice Page for Lamed

Practice writing *lamed*, which has a "l" sound.

ל

Be sure top of letter goes above line.

Stop! Wait until Week 23 to do the rest of this page.

Write the word for *lemon*.

לִמוֹן

Practice writing two more words that begin with *lamed*.

Practice Page for Mem and Final Mem

Practice writing *mem* and *mem sofit*. They have the "m" sound.

 mem

Practice writing the word *flood*.

מַבּוּל

When the mem comes at the end of a word, it looks like this!

final (or sofit) mem

Stop! Do this part in Week 23. You will find many plural words ending with final mem.

See Psalm 23:6 - יָמִים "yah-MEEM," *days*. The word for *day* is יוֹם "yohm," also with a final mem.

Write "yah-MEEM" five times, and "yohm" five times.

Practice Page for Nun

Practice writing *nun* and *nun sofit*. They have an "n" sound.

נ nun

Practice writing the word *Negev* (South).

נֶגֶב

When the nun comes at the end of a word, it looks like this!

nun sofit (final nun)

ן

Stop! Do this in Week 25.

Example of final nun - בְּשֶׁמֶן (vah-SHEH-men), "with oil," Psalm 23:5. Practice writing this ten times.

Practice Page for Samek

Practice writing *samek*, which has a "s" sound as in "snake."

Stop! Do the following exercises in Week 25.
Practice writing the word for *book*.

סֵפֶר

Find two more words that begin with *samek* and write them below.

Practice Page for Ayin

Practice writing *ayin*. It is silent unless it has a vowel point.

Practice the word for *eye*.

עַיִן

Stop! Start this part in Week 27.
Find two more words that start with *ayin* and write them here.

Practice Page for Pay and Fay

Practice writing *pay, fay,* and *fay sofit*.

פּ pay, (with a dot) "p" sound

↓ ↓

פ פ פ.

Write the word for *Pharaoh* (pahr-OH) several times.

פַּרְעֹה

פ fay, (without a dot) "f" sound

↓

פ

Stop! Do this in Week 27.

Example of fay sofit - Genesis 37, יוֹסֵף Joseph (YO-sehf)

Find "Yosehf" in your Tanach (Hebrew O.T. - Genesis 37) and lightly circle in pencil all 14 of them!

ף fay sofit, "f" sound

↓

ף

Practice writing the Hebrew word for *Joseph* several times.

Practice Page for Tsadee

Practice writing *tsadee*, which has a "ts" sound.

tsadee

Write several times the word for *Zion*. צִיּוֹן

Find another word that begins with *tsadee* and write it several times.

Example of tsadee sofit - אֶרֶץ earth, (AH-rets)

final tsadee ץ

Stop! Begin this exercise in Week 29.
Write the word for *earth* below, ten times.

Practice Page for Kuf

Practice writing *kuf*, which has a "k" sound.

ק

Make sure lines do NOT touch. ↗

קוף

Write the word for *monkey* here several times.

Stop! Begin this exercise in Week 29.
Find the word for *holy* and write it here.

Choose another word that begins with *kuf* and write it here.

Practice Page for Reysh

Practice writing *reysh*, which has an "r" sound.

ר

רוֹפֵא

Write the word for *doctor* here.

Stop! Do this exercise in Week 31.
Write two more words that begin with *reysh*.

Practice Page for Sheen and Seen

Practice writing *sheen* and *seen*.

שׁ

sheen (with dot on right)
"sh" sound

Find and write the word for *peace*.

שׂ

seen (with dot on left)
"s" sound

Stop! Do this exercise in Week 31.
Write the word for *field*.

שָׂדֶה

Practice Page for Tahv

Practice writing *tahv*, which has a "t" sound.

Be sure the little "foot" stands out at the bottom!

Practice writing the word *Torah*.

תּוֹרָה

Stop! Do this exercise in Week 33.
Find two words from the picture page that begin with *tahv* and practice them below.

READING PRACTICE

Week 8

Read the first line of letters and vowels, from right to left and top to bottom. Then write the pronunciations for line two. Do the same in each section. Check answers on p. 112.

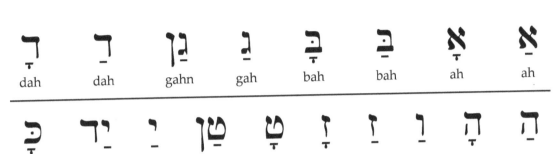

דָ	דַ	נַ	גַ	בָ	בַ	אָ	אַ
dah	dah	gahn	gah	bah	bah	ah	ah

AH

Write out the sounds below each letter.

כָ | יָד | יַ | טַן | טָ | זָ | זַ | הָ | הַ

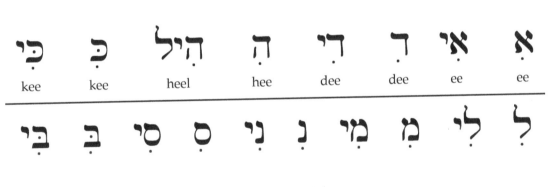

כִי	כִ	הִיל	הִ	דִי	דִ	אִי	אִ
kee	kee	heel	hee	dee	dee	ee	ee

EE

Write out the sounds below each group of letters.

בִּ | בִ | סִ | סִ | נִ | נִי | נ | מִי | מִ | לִי | לִ

טֶ	שֶׁ	רֶ	לֶ	סֶ	פֶּ	בֶּ	אֶ
teh	sheh	reh	leh	seh	peh	beh	eh

EH

Write out the sounds below each letter.

אֶ | טֶ | לֶ | פֶּ | רֶ | דֶ | נֶ | מֶ | גֶ | בֶּ

READING PRACTICE

Week 10

Read the letters with their vowels. Read each letter from top to bottom and right to left. Then fill in the sounds under the letter groups on line two. Do the same for each section.

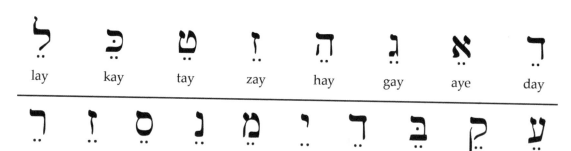

לֵ   כֵּ   טֵ   זֵ   הֵ   גֵ   אֵ   דֵ
lay   kay   tay   zay   hay   gay   aye   day

רֵ   זֵ   סֵ   נֵ   מֵ   יֵ   דֵ   בֵ   קֵ   עֵ

AYE

Write out the sounds below each letter.

סוֹ   רוֹ   פּוֹ   פוֹ   אוֹ   אֹ   לוֹ   לֹ
soh   roh   poh   poh   oh   oh   loh   loh

כֹּ   בּוֹ   גֹ   גוֹ   דוֹ   הֹ   הֹ   זֹ   טוֹ   אוֹ   נוֹ

OH

Write out the sounds below each group of letters.

דוּ   שׁוּ   סוּ   סֻ   כּוּ   לֻ   בֻּ   תֻּ
doo   shoo   soo   soo   koo   loo   boo   too

כֻ   טֻ   זוּ   צוּ   פוּ   נוּ   הוּ   מוּ   גֻ   מֻ

OO

Write out the sounds below each group of letters.

90

READING PRACTICE

Week 13

Read the first line from right to left, top to bottom. Read slowly, making sure you understand.
Then sound out the groups of words in the second row, and write their sounds on the line.

רַב	מַה	מַר	יָם	דָא	גַג	בַּל	אַף
rahv	mah	mahr	yahm	dah	gahg	bahl	ahf

רַק   מַן   מָל   יָד   דָג   גַל   בַּז   טַף

_____

שַׁם	תַּת	שָׁשׁ	קַב	פַּת	עָף	עַז	נָע
shahm	taht	sahs	kahv	paht	ahf	ahz	nah

שַׁל   תָּג   שַׂר   קְט   פַּס   עַל   עַד   נָם

_____

מִידָה	רִיצָה	אִישׁ	בּוֹא	דוֹדָה	פִּיל	הִיא
mee-DAH	ree-TSAH	eesh	boh	doh-DAH	peel	hee

מִילָה   רִיבָּה   אִישָׁה   סוֹד   דוֹד   מִיל   טִיב

_____

Matching Quiz 1

Draw a line in pencil from each picture to the matching Hebrew word.

1. אֶרֶץ

2. בַּיִת

3. אוֹר

4. דָג

5. זְבְרָה

6. כֶּלֶב

7. דְבוֹרָה

8. הַר

Answers on page 112

Matching Quiz 2

Draw a line in pencil from each picture to the matching Hebrew word.

1. גָּמָל

2. גַּן

3. הוֹרִים

4. כַּלָה

5. טַוָוס

6. יֶלֶד

7. בֶּרֶךְ

8. זָהָב

Answers on page 112

Matching Quiz 3

Draw a line in pencil from each picture to the matching Hebrew word.

צִיפּוֹר .1

לִימוֹן .2

לֶחֶם .3

חָתוּל .4

נֵר .5

כִּנוֹר .6

מְנוֹרָה .7

יָד .8

Answers on page 112

Matching Quiz 4

Draw a line in pencil from each picture to the matching Hebrew word.

1. לֵב

2. סוּס

3. עֶצֶם

4. פַּטִּישׁ

5. נֶשֶׁר

6. עֵץ

7. קִיוִי

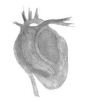

8. סֵפֶר

Answers on page 112

Matching Quiz 5

Draw a line in pencil from each picture to the matching Hebrew word.

1. קוֹף

2. תֻּכִּי

3. רֹאשׁ

4. שֶׁמֶשׁ

5. רֶגֶל

6. תַּפּוּחַ

7. שׁוֹפָר

8. נֵבֶל

Answers on page 112

Names

Fill in the blank with the correct proper names from your reading of the Hebrew. Take your time. Work during weeks 38-40 of the "school year." Can you find these names in your copy of the Hebrew Old Testament (Tanach)? Answers are on page 113.

1. אֲבִינַיִל _____

2. בִּנְיָמִין _____

3. דָּוִד _____

4. דָּן _____

5. הֲדַסָּה _____

6. חַנָּה _____

7. יוֹאֵל _____

8. יוֹסֵף _____

9. יִצְחָק _____

10. לֵאָה _____

11. מִיכָאֵל _____

12. מֹשֶׁה _____

13. נֹחַ _____

14. נְתַנְאֵל _____

15. עִבְרִית _____

16. עָמוֹס _____

17. צִיּוֹן _____

18. רִבְקָה _____

19. רוּת _____

20. רָחֵל _____

21. שְׁמוּאֵל _____

22. שָׁרוֹן _____

Fill-in-blank Quiz 1

These questions are based on the material from the picture pages and the "Notes" in the first section of this book. Make a copy of this quiz BEFORE you take it. Do the quiz the first time on the COPY as an "open book" test, looking up the answers, if needed. Take the quiz a week later without looking up the answers. Check answers on page 113 as a last resort only.

1.   אָדָם (ah-DAHM) means _____.

2.   בַּיִת (BAH-yeet) is _____.

3.   The word meaning "one" is _____. (Write in Hebrew.)

4.   He had five בָּנִים (bah-NEEM) _____.

5.   אוֹר (ore) is the word for _____.

6.   On what day did God create _____ the light? (Hebrew word for "create.")

7.   God placed Adam in a beautiful גַּן (gahn) _____.

8.   The Hebrew word for "rain" is _____.

9.   דֶּלֶת (DEH-let) is a _____.

10. My דּוֹד (dohd) _____ is not exactly rich.

Fill-in-blank Quiz 2

Make a copy of this quiz BEFORE you take the test. Do the quiz the first time on the copy as an "open book" test, looking up the answers, if needed. A week later, take the quiz again without looking up the answers. Always sound out the Hebrew words. Check answers on page 113 as a last resort only.

1. My דָג _____ swims in a big tank.

2. Moses met God up on the _____. (Write in Hebrew.)

3. וָו (Vahv) is a word for _____.

4. הַ (Ha), as a prefix to a word, means "_____."

5. ָ and ַ under a letter sound like "ah," as in the word "_____."

6. זֶבְרָה is a _____.

7. "Silver and זָהָב _____ have I none."

8. The חַתוּל (khah-TOOL) _____ sleeps on the porch.

9. בּוֹקֶר טוֹב (Bo-kehr TOHV) is a greeting for "_____ _____."

10. The יֶלֶד _____ rode his bicycle down the street.

Fill-in-blank Quiz 3

Fill in the blanks. It is recommended that you treat this as an "open book" test. Make a copy of this page BEFORE you take the test. Take the test the first time looking up the answers, if needed. Then, sometime later, take it again without looking up the answers. Check answers on page 113 as a last resort only.

1. The word for "hand" is _____.

2. The כַּלָה _____ was lovely in her white gown.

3. תוּ and תָ can both be pronounced like "_____."

4. Can you count all the כּוֹכָבִים (koh-khah-VEEM) _____?

5. כָּבוֹד is the word for "_____."

6. לֵב is the word for "_____."

7. נָחָשׁ is a _____.

8. King _____ David reigned over Israel for forty years. (Hebrew word for "King.")

9. I like to ride "Beauty," my סוּס _____.

10. The spelling for "blessing" (b'rah-KHA) in Hebrew is _____.

Fill-in-blank Quiz 4

Fill in the blanks. It is recommended that you treat this as an "open book" test. Make a copy of this page BEFORE you take the quiz. Then take it looking up the answers, if necessary. Take it a second time several weeks later, without looking for the answers. Check answers on page 113 as a last resort only.

1. The Hebrew word for "monkey" is _____.

2. The מִצְוָה is a _____, or _____.

3. _____ is the Hebrew word for "elephant."

4. The apostle Paul was let down over the wall in a _____.

5. קֶשֶׁת בֶּעָנָן is a _____, or literally, "a bow in a cloud."

6. It is always enjoyable to read a good _____. (Hebrew word for "book.")

7. "Fruit" and "flower" both begin with the Hebrew letter ____.

8. Moses' wife's name, Zipporah, comes from the Hebrew word _____, meaning "bird."

9. רֹאשׁ means _____ or _____.

10. Write the Hebrew word for "doctor" _____.

Fill-in-blank Quiz 5

Fill in the blanks. It is recommended that you treat this as an "open book" test. Make a copy of this page BEFORE you take the quiz. Take the quiz the first time looking up the answers, if necessary. Take it the second time a week or so later without looking for the answers. Check answers on page 113 as a last resort only.

1. Have you eaten a _____ today? (Hebrew word on Tahv picture page.)

2. A kholam וֹ is a vowel which sounds like the letter ____ as in the word "_____."

3. Gideon blew the _____ (a Bible word for "trumpet.").

4. They say that an olive **tree** _____ can live over a thousand years. (Hebrew word)

5. רוּחַ הַקֹּדֶשׁ means _____, and רוּחַ can also mean _____.

6. "Shalom" is a common greeting in Israel. Spell "Shalom" in Hebrew. _____

7. שׁוֹרֶשׁ means _____.

8. Sometimes a final khaf ךְ is added to a word and stands for the pronoun _____.

9. שֶׁמֶשׁ means _____.

10. In your Tanach, Isaiah 9:6, find the word שַׂר. Is the first letter a "seen" or a "sheen"? _____ The word "sahr" means _____.

102

BIBLE MEMORY VERSES

WEEK 4

בְּרֵאשִׁית בָּרָא אֱלֹהִים אֵת הַשָּׁמַיִם וְאֵת הָאָרֶץ

B'-ray-SHEET bah-RAH Elo-HEEM et ha-shah-MAH-yeem v'et ha-AH-retz.

"In the beginning God created the heavens and the earth." Genesis 1:1

WEEK 11

שְׁמַע יִשְׂרָאֵל יְהוָה אֱלֹהֵינוּ יְהוָה אֶחָד

Sh'MAH Yees-rah-AYL Adoh-NAI Elo-HAY-noo Adoh-NAI eh-KHAD.*

"Hear, O Israel, the LORD our God, the LORD is one." Deuteronomy 6:4 NKJV™

WEEK 21

קָדוֹשׁ קָדוֹשׁ קָדוֹשׁ יְהוָה צְבָאוֹת מְלֹא
כָל־הָאָרֶץ כְּבוֹדוֹ

Kah-DOSH, kah-DOSH, kah-DOSH, Adoh-NAI tsah-vah-OHT. M'-LOW kohl ha-AH-retz k'-VOH-doh.*

..."Holy, holy, holy is the LORD of hosts. The whole earth is full of His glory." Isaiah 6:3 NKJV™

WEEK 31

גַּל־עֵינַי וְאַבִּיטָה נִפְלָאוֹת מִתּוֹרָתֶךָ

Gahl ay-NAI v'ah-BEE-tah neef-lah-OHT me-toh-rah-TEH-kha.

"Open my eyes, that I may see wondrous things from Your law." Psalm 119:18 NKJV™

---

*Why is יהוה translated as "Adonai" and "LORD" here?

The original text of the Hebrew Tanakh had no vowel points. However, the pronunciation for יהוה, the personal name for God, was originally known. Only the high priest spoke the name once a year in the temple, which kept the pronunciation alive at that time. When Titus conquered Jerusalem in 70 A.D., the Jews were taken captive, and the temple was destroyed. Without a temple and a high priest, the pronunciation of יהוה was lost. But even if it were known, to avoid "taking His name in vain," "Adonai," ("my Lord") or "Hashem" ("The Name") is often used by the Jews, and many Bible translators render the name "LORD."

NUMBERS

There is a masculine and a feminine form of the numbers in Hebrew. But we are using only the feminine form here, as this is what is used for IDs, addresses, phone numbers, and counting feminine nouns. When you see capital letters below, this is the syllable to be accented.

WEEK 25

0 - (EH-fes) אֶפֶס

1 - (ah-KHAT) אַחַת

2 - (sh'TAH-yeem) שְׁתַּיִם

3 - (shah-LOSH) שָׁלוֹשׁ

4 - (ar-BAH) אַרְבַּע

5 - (kha-MAYSH) חָמֵשׁ

6 - (shaysh) שֵׁשׁ

7 - (SHAY-vah) שֶׁבַע

8 - (sh'mo-NEH) שְׁמוֹנֶה

9 - (TAY-shah) תֵּשַׁע

10 - (EH-sehr) עֶשֶׂר

WEEK 27

11 - (ah-KHAT es-ray) אַחַת עֶשְׂרֵה

12 - (sh'TAYM es-ray) שְׁתֵּים עֶשְׂרֵה

13 - (sh'-LOSH es-ray) שְׁלוֹשׁ עֶשְׂרֵה

14 - (ar-BAH es-ray) אַרְבַּע עֶשְׂרֵה

15 - (khah-MAYSH es-ray) חֲמֵשׁ עֶשְׂרֵה

16 - (SHAYSH es-ray) שֵׁשׁ עֶשְׂרֵה

17 - (SH'VAH es-ray) שְׁבַע עֶשְׂרֵה

18 - (sh'mo-NEH es-ray) שְׁמוֹנֶה עֶשְׂרֵה

19 - (t'SHAH es-ray) תְּשַׁע עֶשְׂרֵה

20 - (es-REEM) עֶשְׂרִים

WEEK 29

21 - (es-REEM v'-ah-KHAT) עֶשְׂרִים וְאַחַת

22 - (es-REEM oo-sh'-TAH-yeem) עֶשְׂרִים וּשְׁתַּיִם

23 - (es-REEM v'-shah-LOSH) עֶשְׂרִים וְשָׁלוֹשׁ

24 - (es-REEM v'-ar-BAH) עֶשְׂרִים וְאַרְבַּע

25 - (es-REEM v'-kha-MAYSH) עֶשְׂרִים וְחָמֵשׁ

26 - (es-REEM v'-SHAYSH) עֶשְׂרִים וְשֵׁשׁ

27 - (es-REEM vah-SHEH-vah) עֶשְׂרִים וְשֶׁבַע

28 - (es-REEM oo-shmo-NEH) עֶשְׂרִים וּשְׁמוֹנֶה

29 - (es-REEM vah-TAY-shah) עֶשְׂרִים וְתֵשַׁע

30 - (sh'losh-EEM) שְׁלוֹשִׁים

WEEK 35

10 - (EH-sehr) עֶשֶׂר

20 - (es-REEM) עֶשְׂרִים

30 - (sh'losh-EEM) שְׁלוֹשִׁים

40 - (ar-bah-EEM) אַרְבָּעִים

50 - (khah-mee-SHEEM) חֲמִישִׁים

60 - (shee-SHEEM) שִׁשִּׁים

70 - (sheev-EEM) שִׁבְעִים

80 - (sh'mo-NEEM) שְׁמוֹנִים

90 - (teesh-EEM) תִּשְׁעִים

100 - (may-AH) מֵאָה

1,000 - (EH-lef) אֶלֶף

1,000,000 - (meel-YOHN) מִלְיוֹן

COMMON EXPRESSIONS

Good morning! "BO-kehr tohv!" ⇦ בּוֹקֶר טוֹב

Good day! "Yohm tohv!" יוֹם טוֹב

Good night! "LIE-la tohv!" לַיְלָה טוֹב

How are you? (to a male) "Ma shlom-KHA?" מַה שְׁלוֹמְךָ ?

(to a female) "Ma shlo-MEKH?" מַה שְׁלוֹמֵךְ ?

Everything is just fine. - "Bah-RUCH ha-SHEM." (Literally, "Bless the Name") בָּרוּךְ הַשֵּׁם

Fine. "b'-SAY-dehr." בְּסֵדֶר

Very well, thanks very much. "Tohv m'-OHD, toh-DAH rah-BAH." טוֹב מְאֹד תוֹדָה רַבָּה

Please, or, You're welcome. "b'-vak-a-SHA." בְּבַקָּשָׁה

What is your name? (to a male) "Ma-sheem-KHA?" מַה שִׁמְךָ ?

(to a female) "Ma-sh'-MEKH?" מַה שְׁמֵךְ ?

My name is Benjamin Cohen. "Sh'mee Benyamin Cohen." שְׁמִי בְּנְיָמִין כֹּהֵן

My name is Miriam. "Sh'mee Mir'yam." שְׁמִי מִרְיָם

How? - "āych?"	אֵיךְ ?	

How? - "āych?" אֵיךְ ?

What? - "Mah?" מַה ?

When? - "Ma-TIE?" מָתַי ?

Where? - "AY-fo?" אֵיפֹה ?

Why? - "Lah-MAH?" לָמָה ?

Who? - "Mee?" מִי ?

Yes - "Ken" כֵּן

No - "Lo" לֹא

DAYS OF THE WEEK

Sunday - "Yohm ree-SHOHN" יוֹם רִאשׁוֹן

Monday - "Yohm shah-NEE" יוֹם שֵׁנִי

Tuesday - "Yohm sh'-lee-SHEE" יוֹם שְׁלִישִׁי

Wednesday - "Yohm r'-vee-EE" יוֹם רְבִיעִי

Thursday - "Yohm khah-mee-SHEE" יוֹם חֲמִישִׁי

Friday - "Yohm shee-SHEE" יוֹם שִׁישִׁי

Saturday - "Shah-BAHT" שַׁבָּת

105

PERSONAL PRONOUNS

I (either masculine or feminine) אֲנִי ⇦

I am going. (masculine)   אֲנִי הוֹלֵךְ   "Ah-NEE ho-LAYKH."

you (masc. singular) אַתָּה

You are good.   אַתָּה טוֹב   "Ah-TAH tohv."

you (fem. sing.) אַתְּ

You are going to the house.   אַתְּ הוֹלֶכֶת לַבַּיִת   "Aht ho-LEH-khet lah-BAH-yeet."

he, it (m. s.) הוּא

He is strong.   הוּא חָזָק   "Hoo kha-ZAHK."

she, it (f. s.) הִיא

She is pretty.   הִיא יָפָה   "Hee YAH-fah."

we אֲנַחְנוּ

We are eating.   אֲנַחְנוּ אוֹכְלִים   "Ah-NAHKH-noo oh-kh'-LEEM."

you (m. plural) אַתֶּם

אַתֶּם נוֹתְנִים הַרְבֵּה מְאֹד
You are giving much.   "AH-tem no-t'-NEEM har-BAY m'-OHD."

you (f. pl.) אַתֶּן

אַתֶּן לוֹמְדוֹת מִן הַסֵּפֶר
You are learning from the book.   "AH-ten lo-m'-DOHT min ha-SAY-fehr."

they (m. pl.) הֵם

They are standing.   הֵם עוֹמְדִים   "Haym oh-m'-DEEM."

they (f. s.) הֵן

הֵן יוֹשְׁבוֹת עַל הַכִּסְאוֹת
They are sitting on the chairs.   "Hayn yo-sh'-VOHT ahl ha-kee-SOHT."

106

THE VERB "TO BE"

In Hebrew the verbs of "being," such as "am, are, is" are understood by the context of the sentence. You must supply the English when translating. For example:

1. Joseph (is) a man.   יוֹסֵף אִישׁ

2. I (am) a mother.   אֲנִי אִמָּא

3. The man (is) old.   הָאָדָם זָקֵן

4. The boy (is) good.   הַיֶּלֶד טוֹב

5. Today (is) Sunday (liter. first day).*   הַיּוֹם יוֹם רִאשׁוֹן

6. Tomorrow (is) Monday.*   מָחָר יוֹם שֵׁנִי
Circle the "khet" in this sentence. Be sure to give it a gutteral sound when reading aloud.

7. The LORD (is) one.   אֱלֹהִים אֶחָד
Circle the "khet" in this sentence.

For more examples, look on page 52, at Psalm 111, in verse two. It says, "Great (are) the works of the LORD." גְּדֹלִים מַעֲשֵׂי יְהֹוָה This is one of many where you must supply the "being" verb. Can you find more of this kind of example in this Psalm 111, Psalm 34 (page 50), and Psalm 145 (page 53)? Circle each phrase that you find.

Write in Hebrew:

1. Today (is) Friday. _____

2. Tomorrow (is) Saturday. _____
Circle the "khet" in your sentence.

3. She (is) a mother. _____
Check page 106 for personal pronouns.

4. Joseph (is) old. _____

> *Note: In Israel today, the days of the week are simply "First Day, Second Day, Third Day," etc., based on how they are found in the Old Testament. See Exodus 12:15,16; Leviticus 23:7; Numbers 7:12,18,24; I Samuel 30:11; Genesis 1:19; II Chronicles 20:26 and many others.

HOW TO USE JAMES STRONG'S
EXHAUSTIVE CONCORDANCE OF THE BIBLE

A serious student of Hebrew will want to purchase his own copy of James Strong's *Exhaustive Concordance of the Bible*. (Until you are able to purchase a copy, the Reference section of the public library is a good place to become acquainted with "Strong's.") Even before you know how to sound out and read words in Hebrew, this book will be of great value to you. There are several ways to benefit from using this invaluable reference book:

1. In the back section of Strong's *Exhaustive Concordance*, under the title "Hebrew and Chaldee Dictionary Accompanying the Exhaustive Concordance," you may desire to read each entry for the meanings of the Hebrew words.

2. Under the same "Hebrew and Chaldee Dictionary" back section of Strong's reference book, one can find the pronunciation of Hebrew words. It may be helpful to pronounce in the modern Israeli way, however, by saying all tahvs (ת) as a "t" sound, not as "th," and all patakhs (‑) and kamatzes (ָ) as "ah," like in "father."

3. Perusing the "Hebrew and Aramaic [or Chaldee] Dictionary" section is a good way to practice your "alphabetizing," as you would have to do if you looked up an **English** word in an **English** dictionary. This is an excellent drill for getting around in the Hebrew alphabet! The more Hebrew words you look up, the more familiar with the alphabetical order you will be; the faster and easier it becomes to find words.

4. Here is an example which you will probably use a lot: Say you are reading in the English Bible a passage like Psalm 23, and you come to verse six, where it says, "Surely goodness and mercy shall *follow* me all the days of my life..." You are curious to know if the word *follow* has any alternate meanings for a richer understanding. What you need to do first is...

a. Look up in Strong's main concordance under the "f"s, as you would in any dictionary.

b. Next, you see a list of verses with "follow" in them, and you see a column the names of the books of the Bible. You run your eyes down the column until you come to the Psalm 23:6 reference. Part of the verse is quoted, "mercy shall f. me all the days of...," with a number 7291 next to it.

c. Now you are going to turn farther back in the concordance to the Hebrew and Chaldee Dictionary, where all the words are numbered (there are 8,674 of them!). Turn until you find your number for "follow," no. 7291. You see that it reads, "רָדַף (rah-DAHF): a prim. root; to run after; chase, follow after, pursue." You also notice that it says, "(usually with hostile intent)," but your verse is an exception. The verse could be read this way: "Surely goodness and mercy shall pursue [or chase after] me all the days of my life..." Interesting, yes?

> For further study, you might be interested to look up the other Scripture references for "follow" (rah-DAHF), and see how the word is used, and what may be the context or background to the word.

ASSIGNMENT USING JAMES STRONG'S
EXHAUSTIVE CONCORDANCE OF THE BIBLE

1. "It is of the LORD's mercies that we are not consumed, because his compassions fail not. They are **new** every morning: great is thy faithfulness." Lamentations 3:22-23. (KJV)

Use Strong's *Exhaustive Concordance* to look up the word "new" in verse 23.

Question - What are two synonyms that Strong's gives which could be substituted for "new" in verse 23, and still make good sense? Write them on the lines. _____, _____.

Do a little 'detective' work. For instance, when reading about the word "new" in Strong's *Concordance*, when it states "from 2318," be sure to follow the clue! Read all you can about the word "new" for a broader understanding and meaning.

Write Lamentations 3:22-23 with one of the synonyms in the place of the word "new."

_____

_____

2. Using "Strong's" again, look up the word "Sodom." Tell its meaning. _____

_____

3. Do you, or someone you know, have a name that is found in the Old Testament? Look up the name in "Strong's" and write its meaning. Perhaps you will want to look up other names for their meanings. _____

_____

4. "Thou wilt keep him in perfect peace, whose mind is **stayed** on Thee, because he trusteth in Thee." Isaiah 26:3 (KJV) Look up in the *Concordance* the word "stayed" for this verse. The Hebrew word is _____. Write some synonyms for the word "stayed."_____

_____

Rewrite the verse using the synonym of your choice in the place of "stayed." _____

_____

_____

5. First, read II Chronicles 20:1-30. You will notice when reading the passage, that Jehoshaphat and the children of Judah (v.26) "assembled themselves in the valley of Berachah, for there they blessed the LORD: therefore the name of the same place was called, the valley of Berachah unto this day" (KJV).

Assignment: Look up the word "Berachah" in Strong's *Concordance*. It is the Hebrew word numbered 1294. Write "Berachah" in Hebrew. _____. Circle the 3-letter root. The word is a noun meaning the same as #1293: _____. What other word is related to "berachah"? It is the noun pictured on p. 5 of this book. בֶּרֶךְ means _____.

Do you see in this passage a connection with the name "Valley of Berachah" and the word "berekh" (knee)? Read verse 18 again. Could Jehoshaphat and all the people have worshipped the LORD by falling down on their **knees** in supplication and later, thanksgiving?

Compare Psalm 95:6: "O come, let us worship and bow down. Let us kneel before the LORD our maker." What word in this verse is similar to "berachah" of II Chronicles 20:26? _____.

STRONG'S ASSIGNMENT—CONTINUED

5. (Continued.) Check Strong's Concordance.

If you have a Hebrew Interlinear Bible, find the words in II Chronicles 20:26 for "Berachah," and the word "blessed." Circle the 3-letter root in these words.

6. The use of *double verbs* in Biblical Hebrew is an interesting and unique way of expressing an action. It seems that God is emphasizing a point by simply saying it over again: e.g., in Genesis 2:17 He declares, "But of the tree of the knowledge of good and evil you shall not eat, for in the day that you eat of it you shall **surely die**"(NKJV™). But in the Hebrew it is "dying, you shall die." מוֹת תָּמוּת (mote ta-MOOT). Circle the 3-letter roots.

In I Samuel 25:28, Abigail said to David, "I pray thee, forgive the trespass of thine handmaid: for the LORD will **certainly make** my lord a sure house..." (KJV)

What is the Hebrew for "make"? _____ It is Strong's no. _____.

If you look in your Hebrew Interlinear Bible, "certainly make" is עָשֹׂה יַעֲשֶׂה Circle the 3-letter roots for "certainly make."

In the English Old Testament these "doubles" are translated with an adverb such as "freely, surely, greatly, exceedingly, utterly, truly, vividly, certainly, bitterly, grievously, completely, highly, carefully, fiercely, indeed, absolutely," etc.

Here are just a few more "double verbs" in the Tanach:

7. Look up Genesis 2:16. What is the word in Strong's *Concordance* for "eat"? _____.
If you have access to a Hebrew Bible, look up this and the following references. Notice the full verb and adverb as they appear in the Tanach. In this verse, they are אָכֹל תֹּאכֵל Circle the 3-letter roots in these words.
In English, what is the adverb that modifies "eat"? _____

8. Look up Genesis 3:16. What is the word in Strong's *Concordance* for "multiply"? _____.
It is number _____. Be sure to look in a Hebrew Bible to see the double verb. Write it and circle the 3-letter roots. _____ What is the adverb which modifies "multiply"? _____.

9. Look up Micah 2:12. The word in Strong's *Concordance* for "gather" (as in "gather the remnant of Israel") is _____. Strong's number is _____. The double verb in your Hebrew Bible is קַבֵּץ אֲקַבֵּץ Circle the 3-letter roots.
What is the adverb which modifies "gather"? _____.

10. Look up Isaiah 26:3. What kind of peace does the person have whose mind is stayed upon the LORD? _____. Write "shalom, shalom" in Hebrew. _____ _____.
Look "shalom" up in your Tanach or on the שׁ picture page.

Any references or quotes from Strong's *Exhaustive Concordance of the Bible* in this work were taken from the 1890 edition, Abingdon Press, New York, Nashville.

DO YOU RECOGNIZE THIS HEBREW?

This is cursive script, which is used in all writing by hand, e.g., for letters, filling out applications, etc. Read the alef-bet right to left, beginning with alef, at the top. Do you see the final forms of khaf, mem, nun, fay and tsadee?

ANSWERS

Can You Find the A-B-Cs? - Psalm 34, p. 50

First, you will notice that there seems to be the letter vahv (ו) missing in this psalm. You should find it in the middle of verse five as a "shoorook," the vahv with the dot in the middle (וּ). This vahv means "and." So, as it starts a new half verse, "...and their faces were not ashamed," it really is NOT missing! Second, verse 22 repeats the letter pay (פ) and begins the word "redeeming." Why? Study/meditate on the psalm and see if there may be an emphasis on the idea of "redeem."

Can You Find the A-B-Cs?, No. 2 - Psalm 111, p. 52

This psalm has every letter of the Hebrew alef-bet exactly in order, only it does so at every **half** verse!

Can You Find the A-B-Cs?, No. 3 - Psalm 145, p. 53

The only letter missing in the chronological order in this psalm is a nun (נ). Suggestion: See if you can find a "nun verb" in Strong's *Exhaustive Concordance* which has to do with a theme in this psalm. (We suggest the verb נפל) The question "Why is it missing?" is a very intriguing one!

Reading Practice, Week 8, p. 89 (Hebrew letters from right to left)

first row - (ah sounds) ha, ha, vah, zah, zah, tah, tan, yah, yad, kah

second row - (ee sounds) lee, lee, mee, mee, nee, nee, see, see, ee, ee

third row - (eh sounds) beh, geh, meh, neh, deh, reh, peh, leh, tseh, eh

Reading Practice, Week 10, p. 90 (from right to left)

first row - (aye sounds) aye, kay, bay, day, yay, may, nay, say, zay, ray

second row - (oh sounds) boh, boh, goh, goh, doh, hoh, zoh, toh, oh, noh

third row - (oo sounds) moo, goo, moo, hoo, noo, poo, tsoo, zoo, too, koo

Reading Practice, Week 13, p. 91 (from right to left)

first row - tahf, bahz, gahl, dahg, yahd, mahl, mahn, rahk

second row - nahm, ahd, ahl, pahs, kaht, sahr, tahg, shal

third row - teev, meel, dohd, sohd, ee-shah, ree-bah, mee-lah

Matching Quiz 1, p. 92 1. earth 2. house 3. light 4. fish 5. zebra 6. dog 7. bee 8. mountain

Matching Quiz 2, p. 93 1. camel 2. garden 3. parents 4. bride 5. peacock 6. boy 7. knee 8. gold

Matching Quiz 3, p. 94 1. bird 2. lemon 3. bread 4. cat 5. candle 6. violin 7. menorah 8. hand

Matching Quiz 4, p. 95 1. heart 2. horse 3. bone 4. hammer 5. eagle 6. tree 7. kiwi 8. book

Matching Quiz 5, p. 96 1. monkey 2. parrot 3. head 4. sun 5. foot 6. apple 7. shofar 8. harp

ANSWERS—CONTINUED

Names, p. 97   1. Abigail   2. Benjamin   3. David   4. Dan   5. Hadassah (Esther)   6. Hannah   7. Joel   8. Joseph   9. Isaac   10. Leah   11. Michael   12. Moses   13. Noah   14. Nathaniel   15. Hebrew   16. Amos   17. Zion   18. Rebekah   19. Ruth   20. Rachael   21. Samuel   22. Sharon

Quiz 1, p. 98   1. man   2. house   3. אֶחָד   4. sons   5. light   6. בָּרָא   7. garden   8. גֶּשֶׁם   9. door   10. uncle

Quiz 2, p. 99   1. fish   2. הָר   3. hook   4. the   5. many answers: father, papa, mama, etc.   6. zebra   7. gold   8. cat   9. Good morning!   10. boy

Quiz 3, p. 100   1. יָד   2. bride   3. too   4. stars   5. glory   6. heart   7. snake   8. מֶלֶךְ   9. horse   10. בְּרָכָה

Quiz 4, p. 101   1. קוֹף   2. commandment, good deed   3. פִּיל   4. סַל   5. rainbow   6. סֵפֶר   7. פ   8. צִפּוֹר   9. head, chief   10. רוֹפֵא

Quiz 5, p. 102   1. תַּפּוּחַ or תַּפּוּז   2. o, go   3. שׁוֹפָר, shofar   4. עֵץ   5. Holy Spirit, wind   6. שָׁלוֹם   7. root   8. your/thy   9. sun   10. seen, prince

The Verb "To Be," p. 107, Write in Hebrew: 1. Today is Friday. הַיּוֹם יוֹם שִׁישִׁי
2. Tomorrow is Saturday. מָחָר שַׁבָּת   3. She is a mother. הִיא אִמָּא
4. Joseph is old. יוֹסֵף זָקֵן

Assignment Using *Strong's Exhaustive Concordance*, pp. 109-110.

1. fresh, renewed; "It is of the LORD'S mercies that we are not consumed, because His compassions fail not. They are fresh (or renewed) every morning; great is Thy faithfulness."

2. "Sodom" means scorched, volcanic or bituminous; a place near the Dead Sea.   3. Your answer.

4. sah-MAHKH - סָמַךְ; synonyms - leaning, resting, taking hold upon, standing fast. Isaiah 26:3: "Thou wilt keep him in perfect peace, whose mind is leaning (resting, taking hold) on thee, because he trusteth in thee."   5. בְּרָכָה; prosperity, blessing; knee; kneel.

6. "Make" is עָשָׂה "ah-SAH"; Strong's no. 6213.

7. אָכַל "ah-KHAL"; freely.

8. "Multiply" is רָבָה, "rah-VAH," no. 7235; הַרְבָּה אַרְבֶּה; greatly.

9. קָבַץ "ka-BAHTS"; Strong's no. 6908; surely.

10. Isaiah 26:3 - perfect; שָׁלוֹם שָׁלוֹם

113

CREDITS

(Alphabetized by last name or title—Inclusion in this list does not imply endorsement of any website, book, etc.)

13th century Jewish artist living in France
Drawing of "David," Dalet page.

Aichinger, Robert
Photos of "book," Samek page and pgs. 89-91; "sun," Sheen page.

Amstrup, Steve, U.S. Fish and Wildlife Service
Photo of "bear," Dalet page.

Andres Forero, Daniel
Photo of "turtle," Tsadee page.

Baldridge, Shelley
Photo of Jordan River (bottom banner), Yud page.

Baranski, Krzysztof
Photo of "peacock," Tet page.

Berkompas, Benjamin
Photo of "bird," Tsadee page.

Bible Cyclopaedia, by Rev. A. R. Fausset, M.A., 1892
Illustration of "olives," Zayin page.

Book of Hours, Ms. Library of Congress. Rosenwald ms. 10
Painting of "scribe" (modified), Samek page.

Borchard, Alfred
Photos used as banners, Bet page.

Boulanger, Martin
Photo of leaf (top banner), Ayin page.

Brough, Colin
Photo of garden, p. 93.

Brown, Gareth J.
Photo of "elephant," Pay page.

Burgess, Janet
Photo of "window," Khet page.

de Bruyne, Danny
Photo of "snake," Nun page.

C., Andrew
Background papers and textures, Tahv facing page.

Carollo, Christian
Photo of "tree," Ayin page.

Christner, Benjamin
Photo of "bride," Kaf page.

Cody, Moi
Illustration of horse, p. 95.

Dembinski, Dariusz
Photo of "forest," Yud page.

DeLadurantey, Hannah
Photo of "clarinet," Kuf page; harpist on Nun facing page.

Dictionary of The Holy Bible, by William W. Rand, D.D., 1914
Map used on bottom and top banners, Alef page.

Die biblischen Altertümer, by Paul Volz, 1914
Image of "chariot" (Based on an Egyptian relief), Mem page.

Dorsett, Marc
Photo of "organ," Ayin page.

Empey, Cheryl
Photo of rainbow (banners), Kuf page.

Erdos, David
Photo of the Eastern Gate (bottom banner), Sheen page.

Firus, Henry (of Flagstaffotos)
Photo of "wheel," Gimel page.

Ford Elliott, Steve
Photo of "rooster," Tahv page.

Gabriel, Jeannine
Photo of "grapevine," Gimel page.

Gobart, Grace
Oil paintings of "ship," Alef page; "fish," Dalet page.

Gobart, Michael
Photo used on top banner, Hay page.

Gómez Soberano, Jose Alfredo
Photo of "scarf, veil," Tsadee page.

de Graaf, Hilda
Photo of "bracelet," Tsadee page.

gracey (on http://morguefile.com)
Top banner on Tsadee page.

Hodgson, Chris
Photo of "caterpillar," (modified), Zayin page.

http://imageafter.com/
Photos of "gate" and "root," Sheen page.

Kirby, Roger
Photo of "door," Dalet page.

Linder, Robert
Photo used for "create," Bet page.

Lobeck, Nick
Photo of "bone," Ayin page.

Manteufel, Jillian
Drawings of "dog," Kaf page; "raccoon," Reysh page; dog on Matching Quiz 1 page.

Mears, D
Photo of "monkey," Kuf page.

Meirlaen, Lies
Photo of monkey, p. 96.

Merritt, Alyse (www.tendershootfilms.com)
Watercolors of "menorah," Mem page; "fruits," Pay page.

Merritt, Andrew
Drawings of "giraffe," Gimel page; "mouse," Ayin page.

Merritt, Ann
Watercolors of "flag," Dalet page; "prayer shawl," Tet page; "dreidal," Samek page; photos of "eating" (Nathaniel Merritt), Alef page; "garden," Gimel page; "uncle" (Marshall Merritt), Dalet page; "palace" and "the chair," Hay page; banners, Vahv page; banners and "gold," Zayin page; "friends," "cat," "arrow," and "beetle," Khet page; "teapot," Tet page; "boy" (Luke Holbrook), "diamond," and "vegetable," Yud page; "violin," Kaf page; banners, "bread," "lioness," and "lemon," Lamed page; "key," "matzah," and "fountain," Mem page; "harp," Nun page; "cup," "salad," and top banner, Samek page; bottom banner, "tomato," and "eyes," (Elizabeth Merritt's), Ayin page; "flower," "butterfly," and "piano," Pay page; "radish" and "frog," Tsadee page; "kiwi," "shell," "cinnamon," and "potter," Kuf page; bottom banner, Pay page; "head," (Amarisa Merritt's); "shepherd" and "pomegranate," Reysh page; top banner, Sheen page; top banner, "corn," "orange," "apple," "parrot," and "palm tree," Tahv page; photo of bird, p. 94. Photograph of old book on the back cover.

CREDITS

Merritt, John (www.tendershootfilms.com)
  Photo of "camel," Gimel page.

Merritt, Mary
  Photos of "daughters" and "sons," Bet page; "hush," Hay page; "foot," Reysh page. Drawings of "Henay Ma Tov"/Psalm 133 song, Tet facing page; "Ha Tikva" song, Tahv page; "heart," p. 95; hands, p. 64 and p. 66, and Hebrew cursive letters, p.110. Watercolor of "seahorse," Samek page.

Merritt, Matthew (www.redbubble.com/people/mmerritt)
  Photos of "lightning," Bet page; sunset banners, Tet page; "moon," Yud page; "night," Lamed page; "tiger," Nun page; top banner of Pay page.

Merritt, Melissa (http://paintermelissa.wordpress.com)
  All full-page watercolors in this book are by Melissa Merritt. The scrolls on each page were also painted by Melissa. Other watercolors by Melissa: The Lion's Gate, scroll, and stone tablets on cover. The Damascus Gate and Eastern Gate, Sheen facing page, "earth" and "light," Alef page; "onion," "knee," and "behemoth/beast," Bet page; "cheese" and "rain," Gimel page; banners on Dalet page; "Hadassah (Esther)," Hay page; hook, light, the ark, and Adam and Eve, Vahv page; "milk," Khet page; "chef," Tet page; handshake, Tet facing page; "hand" and "dove," Yud page; "crown" and "symbols," Kaf page; "whale/leviathan," Lamed page; "commandment" and "king," Mem page; banners and "candle," Nun page; "basket," Samek page; "pearl" and "hammer," Pay page; "doctor," Reysh page, and Torah scroll, Tahv page. Photos of "bee," Dalet page; "zebra," Zayin page; "dessert," Mem page; "basket," Samek page; "mouth," Pay page; and "jam," Reysh page. Image of a man walking, p. 62, based on a Scott Liddell photo.

Meyer, Claudia
  Photo of "lotus," Lamed page.

Mleczko, Pawel
  Photo used on bottom banner, Hay page.

Morawiec, Marcin
  Photo of "ant," Nun page.

Moschetti, Viola
  Photo of "river," Nun page.

NASA, ESA, and The Hubble Heritage Team (STScI/AURA), Acknowledgment: N. Smith (University of California, Berkeley) (http://hubblesite.org/gallery/)
  Photos used on banners, Kaf page.

NASA, ESA, and the Hubble Heritage Team (STScI/AURA), -ESA/Hubble Collaboration. Acknowledgment: D. Gouliermis (Max Planck Institute for Astronomy, Heidelberg)
  Photo of "stars," Kaf page.

NASA, ESA and A. Nota (STScI/ESA)
  Photo used on bottom banner, Kaf page.

natascha_rausch@yahoo.com (via http://www.morguefile.com)
  Photo of "watch," Sheen page.

Nelson, Lillian
  Photo used on bottom banner (feathers), Tsadee page.

Nijhuis, Patrick
  Photo of "photographer," Tsadee page.

Our Day: In the Light of Prophecy, By W.A. Spicer
  Illustration of man preaching, p. 65.

Pavlakovic, Mira
  Photo used on top banner, Reysh page.

Pearson Scott Foresman (educational publisher)
  Illustration of "crocodile," Tahv page.

Peloubet's Select notes on the International Sunday School Lessons
  Illustrations of "mountain," (by John Huybers) and "Hallelu/Praise," Hay page, "rings," Tet page; "Western wall," Kaf page; "menorah," used on cover and Mem page banners; Scrolls and pens used on bottom banner, Tahv page; tree, p. 95.

Preda Struteanu, Mircea
  Photo of "eagle," Nun page.

Renoir, Pierre-Auguste
  Oil painting of "girl" (Girl with Watering Can), Yud page.

Reynolds, Sir Joshua
  Oil painting of "The Infant Samuel" (modified), Hay page.

Richert, Christa
  Photo of "willow," Tsadee page.

Ruellan, Gabriela
  Photo of "feather," Nun page.

Sawyer, Jane M.
  Photo of "rainbow," Kuf page; bottom banner, Samek page.

Scheijen, Jean
  Photo of "nest," Kuf page.

Schneider, Barbara
  Photo of "ostrich," Yud page.

Serna, Eva
  Photo used on bottom banner (Petra), Reysh page.

Short Family, The (http://homeandheritagedesigns.com)
  Photo of "sheep," Kaf page.

St. John, Carrie
  Photo of "family" (Keith Merritt and family), Hay page.

St. John, Leslie and Connie
  Photo of "house" ("Frey Place," Palatine Bridge, NY), Bet page.

Tallent, Mike and Alecia
  Photo of "sword," Khet page.

Theodore Beza's "Icones"
  Illustration of John Knox, used for "beard," Zayin page.

U.S. Fish and Wildlife Service
  Photo of "wolf," Zayin page.

Unknown photographers and illustrators
  Photos of "father," "mother," and "man," (Keith Merritt, the author's husband), Alef page; "aunt" (Elsie Merritt), Dalet page. Banner of Jerusalem, Yud page.

vintageprintable (via http://www.flickr.com)
  Illustration of "bat," Ayin page. This work is licensed under the Creative Commons Attribution 2.0 Generic License. To view a copy of this license, visit http://creativecommons.org/licenses/by/2.0/

Vogt, Mary R.
  Photos of "wind," Reysh page, and "horse," Samek page.

W., Billy (aka NoShoes on http://www.sxc.hu)
  Photo of "heart," Lamed page.

Wright, Ted
  Photo of "cake," Ayin page.

Zacharzewski, Michal
  Photo of "kid, baby goat," Gimel page, and peacock, p. 93.

ACKNOWLEDGMENTS

First, I wish to thank Dr. D. Michael Michael for his genuine interest in this book and for his invaluable help with editing. As an instructor in Hebrew and a native Israeli, I knew I could count on him for excellent insight into the language. I thank God for Dr. Michael's help, as this project might never have been completed without his ready advice!

Many thanks to Sara Purcell of Texas for her kindness in serving as "extra eyes" in editing. Her knowledge of Hebrew is brilliant!

To my two daughters, Ann and Melissa Merritt, I am deeply indebted. Annie, you did an excellent job in book layout and fixing all the things that I had no idea how to do! Melissa, what would this project be without your super watercolor pictures? Thank you, girls, so much!

To Kristina Fowl from San Antonio, Texas, I extend my gratitude, as she went through the book as a Hebrew student and found it helpful and satisfying.

A great big THANK YOU goes to my daughter-in-law, Alyse Merritt, who got me started learning the Hebrew alef-bet in the first place!

A big "thank you" to ALL of you people who had a part in photography, paintings, or encouragement. May God bless each of you!

- Mary A. Merritt

About the Author

Mary Alice Merritt holds a Master's Degree in Music Education from Ithaca College, Ithaca, New York. After her husband, Keith, and she taught their eight children at home from 1976 to 2001, Mary began her study of the Hebrew language. Her principle books of study were *Biblical Hebrew, Step by Step*, by Menahem Mansoor, *Contemporary Hebrew*, by Menahem Mansoor, a Hebrew-English Interlinear Bible, James Strong's *Exhaustive Concordance of the Bible*, and a couple of good Hebrew dictionaries. She also benefited much from the Hebrew classes at Beth Israel Sephardic Congregation in Florida, as well as various online study programs. She will always be indebted to Dr. D. Michael Michael of Tampa, Florida, a teacher of Hebrew across the U.S.A. and in Israel, for his invaluable instruction and helps.

Mary claims that "learning largely on your own can be very challenging, yet extremely rewarding. Anyone with a few good helps, a desire to learn, and the blessing of the Lord, can get a good grasp of the language and find fulfillment and great satisfaction in searching the Old Testament."

Mary resides in Texas with a son and two daughters and enjoys twelve grandchildren.

About the Editor

Dr. D. Michael Michael was born in Haifa, Israel, in 1943, and first came to the United States of America as a foreign exchange student in 1960. After several years of attending church and Bible studies, he was changed by the Holy Spirit to follow Jesus as his Messiah and Lord. In 1963, as a permanent resident of the U.S.A., Dr. Michael was drafted into the Army and served as combat chaplain in Vietnam from '64 to '68. In '73 he returned to Israel as a volunteer in the Israeli Defense Forces during the recapture of Jerusalem.

Over the years, Dr. Michael's knowledge of the Hebrew language qualified him to teach in various Jewish schools, synagogues and churches, both in Israel and the United States. He currently teaches Hebrew studies at the Tampa Theological Seminary and Christian College in Tampa, Florida. He leads tours to Israel each year in serving the Israeli Defense Forces.

Dr. Michael lives in Tampa, Florida, with his wife, MaryDee. They have a daughter living in Florida, a son in Israel, and have three grandchildren.

Hebrew:

BEGINNING YOUR JOURNEY

is available at:

olivepresspublisher.com

amazon.com

barnesandnoble.com

and other websites.

Book stores and book distributors may obtain this book through:

Ingram Book Company

or by e-mailing

olivepressbooks@gmail.com

You may contact the author at:

BeginningHebrew@yahoo.com

Milton Keynes UK
Ingram Content Group UK Ltd.
UKHW050383230923
4291660UK00009B/67